Narrative of My Captivity
among the Sioux Indians

Respectfully
Fanny Kelly

NARRATIVE OF MY CAPTIVITY AMONG THE SIOUX INDIANS

By
Fanny Kelly

EDITED BY
CLARK AND MARY LEE SPENCE

KONECKY&KONECKY

T 121459

Konecky & Konecky
150 Fifth Ave.
New York, NY 10011

ISBN: 1-56852-244-4

Frontispiece illustration courtesy of
American Heritage Center, University of Wyoming

Printed and bound in the USA

CONTENTS

ILLUSTRATIONS

PROLOGUE

SHORTLY before dusk on July 12, 1864, a band of
Oglala Sioux attacked a small wagon train near
the Little Box Elder Creek in Wyoming, killing
three men, wounding two others, and carrying away
two children and two women, one of whom was
Fanny Kelly. She would remain a captive for the
next five months.

Here is the account of her trials, her ordeal,
which ended when a party of the Blackfeet Sioux,
under pressure from the army, brought her safely
to Fort Sully in Dakota Territory. "Am I free, indeed free?" Fanny asked, almost in disbelief.

Physically, she was indeed free, but the memories
of those dark and difficult months would no doubt
haunt her for the rest of her life. Only a woman of
strong character could have survived the trauma
and the anguish of what she experienced. An effort
to dramatically describe the abrupt turnabout in
Fanny's life is reflected in the preface to an 1872
edition of her book which excitedly proclaims:

Reader ... ponder the situation. A young and tender
woman following the fortunes of her loving and beloved husband into the great desert, the Land of Promise far in the distance, dreams of wealth and future
happiness. The man of God, who is in the party, now
sharing in the labors of the journey, now preaching
a sermon, offering prayers for the well-being of all, or
"singing a song of the Lord in a strange land." The

playful gambols of the children, the high-wrought
hopes animating all; all rudely interrupted by the rifles
of the merciless savages, most of the men cruelly murdered—the two ladies, and the female child spared,
doubtlessly for a fate worse than death—the heroic
authoress choosing to abandon the tender and adored
child in the desolate waste, a prey to wolves, jackals,
and reptiles, rather than rear her for her inevitable
fate. Think of the trials, the privations, the awful uncertainty, the harrowing fears, the mourning after her
lost child, the torturing uncertainty as to the fate of
her husband, the constant gnawings of hunger, the
sudden transfer of a carefully reared lady from all the
surroundings of refinement to the loathsome, sickening, debasing life of the wildest savages; imagine her
longing, mourning retrospect during those dreary
months—cold, in a starving condition. . . . [1]

Like the women in general who helped build the
West, young Fanny Kelly was tough-minded, re-
sourceful and resilient. She played a more dramatic
role than most of her pioneering sisters, and wrote
about it to a broad national audience. This book is
her story, a real life drama played out in the western wilds against a backdrop of intensifying Indian-
white ferocity.

*   *

Relations between Indians and the whites were
relatively peaceful in the West during the first half
of the nineteenth century. To be sure, there had
been raids and even battles, but not full-scale continuing war. Beaver hunters offered no real threat to

[1] Fanny Kelly, *Narrative of My Captivity among the Sioux
Indians* (Toronto, 1872), pp. vii–viii.

the Indian way of life. Only when sizable wagon trains of permanent settlers began heading for Oregon and California in the early 1840s did the Native Americans begin seriously to fear white encroachment. After 1849, the greatly expanded migration of gold-seekers through Indian terrain only sharpened that apprehension.

In 1851, thanks to the fine work of Indian agent Thomas Fitzpatrick, the federal government concluded the Treaty of Fort Laramie with delegates of various tribes, including the Sioux, Cheyenne, Crow, and Arapahoe, which in theory defined the boundaries of tribal lands and established the prospect of peaceful transit along the Overland Trail. But the real world was more difficult. Unfortunate clashes did occur and indeed multiplied. In August, 1854, the combination of a brash, inexperienced young officer, Lieutenant John L. Grattan, and his drunken interpreter precipitated a quarrel over the killing of a traveler's straggling cow by Sioux near Fort Laramie into an open confrontation that resulted in the deaths of Grattan and twenty-nine of his men.[2]

Defiant and angry, the Sioux scattered to the upper Missouri, raiding settlers and travelers alike. In

[2] Howard R. Lamar, ed., *The Reader's Encyclopedia of the American West* (New York, 1977), pp. 460–61. See Leroy R. Hafen and Francis Marion Young, *Fort Laramie and the Pageant of the West, 1834–1890* (Lincoln, Nebr., 1984 ed.), pp. 221–32; Lloyd E. McCann, "The Grattan Massacre," *Nebraska History*, XXXVII (March, 1956), pp. 1–25.

retaliation, a year later a punitive expedition under General William S. Harney marched up the Overland Trail and attacked the camp of Brulé Sioux near Ash Hollow in western Nebraska, destroying the village and killing more than a hundred men, women and children.[3] After this demonstration of power, Harney marched triumphantly through the Sioux lands and dictated a stern peace to nine assembled tribes at Fort Pierre in 1856. This may have quieted the Sioux for a time, although it took two subsequent campaigns in 1857 and 1858 to quell the Cheyennes; but in reality Harney's action was simply the opening gun of the first major challenge to the mighty Sioux on the northern plains. Without any doubt, there existed a general Indian hostility which was so clear-cut that by the close of the fifties "one could speak of a Plains Indian barrier of Sioux, Cheyennes, Arapahoes, Kiowas, and Comanches extending from the Mexican to the Canadian border."[4]

Soon new forces would exacerbate the differences between the two races. A bloody Sioux uprising in Minnesota in 1862 would have serious ramifications for all the Indians in the upper Missouri Basin.

[3] Lamar, *Reader's Encyclopedia*, pp. 485–86; Hafen and Young, *Fort Laramie*, pp. 239–44; Eugene Bandel, *Frontier Life in the Army, 1854–1861* (edited by Ralph Bieber, Glendale, Calif., 1932), pp. 29–36.

[4] Francis Paul Prucha, *The Great Father: The United States Government and the American Indians* (Lincoln, Nebr., 1984), I, p. 350.

And gold discoveries on the South Platte and in assorted nooks and crannies of the Inland Empire—Washington, Oregon, Idaho and Montana—would bring hordes of gold-seekers scurrying across Indian lands, and pressures to establish more military forts and to force new treaties upon the tribes.

The early sixties were years of the sprawling, restless mining frontier. California mining had moved from placer to more prosaic hard rock or hydraulic mining by that time. The elusive pull of precious yellow metal cast countless prospectors adrift to ransack the canyons and the high mountain valleys of most of the Far West, to penetrate the most remote regions. The virus of gold fever was as incurable as it was contagious. A few nuggets or a small poke of dust panned from some icy stream spawned hell-roaring camps, alive with humanity overnight. "What a clover field is to a steer," wrote an Oregon columnist in 1862, "the sky to the lark—a mudhole to a hog, such are new diggings to a miner."[5]

Nevada was the legitimate heir of California. Emigrants bound for California found limited amounts of gold in the Washoe Mountains, but cursed that "damned blue stuff" that clogged their rockers. In time, assayers identified the "damned blue stuff" as silver and in 1859 the rush was on to Washoe—"Root Hog or Die"—and raw, boisterous Virginia

[5] Quoted in William J. Trimble, *The Mining Advance into the Inland Empire* (Madison, Wisc., 1914), p. 158.

City boomed and awaited development of the great Comstock Lode.[6]

Meanwhile, another chapter was being written in the Colorado Rockies, where in the summer of 1858 enough pay dirt was discovered to send the call of "Gold" echoing east in ever-widening circles. Of the thousands who responded, most were disappointed, but a year later new strikes would clog the routes along the Platte, the Smoky Hill and the Arkansas as camps like Idaho Springs, Black Hawk and Gold Hill boomed.[7]

Farther north, British Columbia's Fraser River mines had beckoned in 1858. Two years later miners prospecting as they returned hit gold on the Clearwater in what would become Idaho. From the swarming new camps at Pierce City and Orofino, a floating population spilled over onto the Salmon River in 1861–62, making a reason to redraw treaty lines since the gold was on Indian lands. To the south, beginning in 1862, prospectors stampeded into the rich placers of Boise Basin and a year later,

[6]See Grant H. Smith, *The History of the Comstock Lode, 1850–1920* (University of Nevada Bulletin Vol. 37, No. 3, Geology & Mining Series 37, Reno, Nevada, 1943). Other excellent sources for the western mining frontiers in general include Rodman W. Paul, *Mining Frontiers of the Far West* (New York, 1963); William S. Greever, *The Bonanza West: The Story of the Western Mining Rushes, 1848–1900* (Norman, Okla., 1963); and Otis E. Young, Jr., *Western Mining* (Norman, Okla., 1970).

[7]See Phyllis F. Dorset, *The New Eldorado: The Story of Colorado's Gold and Silver Rushes* (New York, 1970).

newspapers noted a "special forty-eight-hour insanity for Owyhee," a new district in the southwestern part of the territory.[8]

East of the mountains, eager Coloradans heading for north Idaho in 1862 found gold on Grasshopper Creek, where lusty Bannack City[9] attracted stampeders by the thousands. Eleven months later prospectors hit it big in Alder Gulch, seventy-five miles away, and Virginia City boomed. Finally, in the summer of 1864, came the strikes at Last Chance Gulch—Helena—just two months after the Territory of Montana had been carved out of Idaho.[10]

All of this new activity had a profound impact on Indian-white relations in the early sixties. The shortest overland routes to Colorado, Idaho and Montana led directly across lands guaranteed to the various tribes. To the north, the long, winding lifeline of the Missouri River cut through the heart of Indian territory. This surge of travel coincided with increasing ferment as a result of the Sioux uprising in Minnesota and the withdrawal of regular army troops from the West to fight in the Civil War.

[8]See Trimble, *Mining Advance*; Merle W. Wells, *Gold Camps and Silver Cities* (Idaho Bureau of Mines & Geology Bulletin 22, Moscow, Idaho, 1963), and Wells, *Rush to Idaho* (Idaho Bureau of Mines & Geology Bulletin 19, Moscow, Idaho, no date).

[9]Bannack was the Kelly's announced destination before their wagon train was attacked.

[10]Greever, *The Bonanza West*, 216–21; Michael P. Malone and Richard B. Roeder, *Montana: A History of Two Centuries* (Seattle, 1976), pp. 50–69.

The years 1861–65 were critical times for the West and for the nation at large. The United States was engaged in the worst internal conflict in its history just at a time when the Plains Indians were becoming alarmingly distressed at the growing number of emigrant wagon trains, numerous stagecoaches, and a worsening invasion of intruders. Already the vast seas of buffalo, the red man's way of life, had started to fade. As the Union Pacific Railroad slowly began to push westward, professionals like William F. Cody slaughtered them by the thousands to feed the rail crews and soon the hide hunters would not be far behind.

Many Indians saw the implications for them by this time; the good old days were gone, replaced by greedy interlopers who brought with them firewater, disease and plows. The young braves especially grew angry and watched each incursion with growing concern over their own precarious situation. More and more they believed that if they were to survive, they must take a stand against the invaders.

The period of the Civil War provided an excellent opportunity. Scattered western settlements were thinly guarded and vulnerable during the war years. Most of the federal army was involved in the war in the East, with only light armament available elsewhere. Western areas had to rely mainly on volunteer troops with nondescript weapons or as the war progressed on "Galvanized Yankees," paroled Confederate prisoners who volunteered to fight the

Indians. But despite mounting unrest, during the Civil War the Indians remained comparatively passive, except for numerous local raids and one major upheaval—the uprising of the Santee Sioux in Minnesota during 1862.

This tragic and bloody event erupted from underlying resentment over half a century of white encroachment on their lands, the seduction of Indian women by unprincipled whites, deceptive dealing by corrupt white traders and federal agents, and the devastating impact of the white man's booze. Rage and frustration led up to the murder of five whites by a small band of Sioux near New Ulm, Minnesota in mid-August, 1862. Panic stricken survivors bolted into the towns, spreading exaggerated stories of a general Indian insurrection. Equally as surprised over the murders and well aware of the inevitable white reaction, the Minnesota Sioux concluded that they must either fight or flee. Some prepared for war; others headed west. Little Crow and some 1,300 warriors remained and quickly took the offense, attacking outlying settlements of the Minnesota River Valley, burning barns and houses, killing some 737 men, women and children and taking hundreds more prisoner. War swept southern Minnesota. The Sioux routed volunteers, nearly captured Fort Ridgley and almost overran New Ulm before local militia under popular Colonel Henry Sibley defeated them. Large numbers of the Sioux fled to the Dakotas, taking numerous hostages with them. Capturing more than 1,700 prisoners, the army conducted a gigantic court-martial and condemned 300 of them to death, but through the intervention of President Lincoln, all but thirty-eight of the death sentences were commuted. In late December, Mankato residents observed the simultaneous hanging of the thirty-eight; all from a single scaffold. "America's greatest mass execution," a spectator called it, as the Minnesota Sioux episode came to a lethal close.[11]

The next year a two-pronged punitive expedition, one column under Colonel Sibley and one under General Alfred Sully, chastised the Sioux with moderate success. From newly established Fort Sully on the Missouri River, a few miles below Pierre, and from a supply base at recently-built Fort Rice ten miles north of the Missouri's junction with the Cannonball River, General Sully marched west in the fall of 1864 with 2,200 men across Dakota along the Cannonball and Heart Rivers. He had reliable reports regarding the massing of from 5,000 to 6,000 Hunkpapas, Blackfeet, Yanktonais, Miniconjous,

[11] Lamar, *Reader's Encyclopedia*, pp. 749–50; Dee Brown, *Bury My Heart at Wounded Knee* (New York, 1972 ed.), pp. 38–65. For a contemporary description, see the *Lakeside Classics* volume, Harriet E. Bishop McConkey, *Dakota War Whoop: Indian Massacres and War in Minnesota*, edited by Dale L. Morgan (Chicago, 1965). Kenneth Carley, *The Sioux Uprising of 1862* (St Paul, Minn., 1961), is brief but balanced, while a detailed, fully documented account can be found in William Watts Folwell, *A History of Minnesota* (St Paul, Minn., 1924), II, pp. 109–264.

Sans Arc and the troublesome Santee Sioux in the vicinity of the Little Missouri Bad Lands. With devastating artillery fire, the troops crushed the Indians at Tahkahoukuty, or Killdeer Mountain, then destroyed all their homes—some 1,600 of them—and their precious food supplies. This was the battle which Fanny Kelly viewed and heard during her captivity. Two weeks later, hostilities were taken up again, as General Sully moved through the Bad Lands, killing a hundred Indians in a march that involved not only constant skirmishing, but scorching summer heat, and a scarcity of both rations and water. As a result of this major offensive, the dispossessed Minnesota Sioux as well as their western kinsmen, including the Oglalas, faced a year of cold, misery, disease and starvation.[12]

In the aftermath of the Minnesota Sioux bloodbath, the Platte River route became more dangerous, especially east of South Pass, and by 1864 the thousands of emigrants who headed west along the "Nebraska Coast," as the Platte was occasionally called, found themselves in much more peril than those of earlier migrations. Indians raided ranches, stations, and isolated small wagon trains, while troops in turn pursued the hostiles. These small scale skirmishes increased, especially in 1863 and

[12]See Robert M. Utley, *Frontiersmen in Blue: The United States Army and the Indian 1848–1865* (New York, 1967), pp. 275–80; and Langdon Sully, *No Tears for the General: The Life of Alfred Sully, 1821–1879* (Palo Alto, Calif., 1974), pp. 180–97.

1864, when John Bozeman began to lead emigrants diagonally across Wyoming through prime Indian hunting grounds east of the Big Horn Mountains in a short-cut to the Montana diggings. The advent of this Bozeman Trail in subsequent years required a line of three new forts for protection and would goad the Sioux to take the warpath and force the closing of the route in 1868.[13]

Farther south, the Cheyennes and Arapahoes continually raided trail-users, seeking horses and weapons. By the summer of 1864, they had control of lines of communication east of Denver and large scale attacks on Colorado settlements were contemplated. Eventually, late in November, Colonel John M. Chivington, the "Fighting Parson," and about 750 men of the Third Colorado Volunteers fell upon the peaceful village of Black Kettle's Cheyennes at Sand Creek and brutally slaughtered some 150 Indians—men, women and children.[14]

This was the setting into which Fanny Kelly, her family and her fellow travelers, lured by the bright opportunities to be found in Bannack City, left

[13]See Grace Raymond Hebard and E. A. Brinistool, *The Bozeman Trail*, 2 vols. (Cleveland, 1922); Dorothy M. Johnson, *The Bloody Bozeman: The Perilous Trail to Montana's Gold* (New York, 1971).

[14]A personal account of this episode is found in another *Lakeside Classics* volume, William M. Breakenridge, *Helldorado: Bringing the Law to the Mesquite*, edited by Richard Maxwell Brown (Chicago, 1982), pp. 29–59. See also Utley, *Frontiersmen in Blue*, pp. 293–97 and Stan Hoig, *The Sand Creek Massacre* (Norman, Okla., 1961).

their established homes on May 17, 1864 for the Territory of Idaho, which in ten days would be subdivided to create the new Territory of Montana.

As they set out over one of the standard routes, crossing the country of the recalcitrant Sioux at a time the Indians were unruly and uneasy, one has to wonder how much the Kellys knew about the Indian situation at the time. It was the luck of the draw that they, of the 40,000 who passed along the Platte route that year, became unwitting victims of the Sioux unrest.

*   *

Born either in 1842 or 1845 in Orillia, on the shores of Lake Simcoe in Ontario, Canada, Fanny Kelly was one of two daughters and two sons of James and Margaret Wiggins.[15] Caught up in the fervent land hunger and expansionism that gripped the United States in the mid-nineteenth century, Wiggins in 1856 joined a New York abolitionist colony led by Ephraim Fisk which combined with another guided by Merritt Moore of Michigan to form the Union Settlement Association in eastern Kansas. Wiggins traveled to the site of the proposed new community of Geneva in northwest Allen County, above the Neosho River, and went back for his family the following year. Unfortunately, on the return

---

[15] For an excellent, carefully researched account of the life and ordeal of Fanny Kelly, see Randy Brown, "Attack on the Kelly-Larimer Wagon Train," *Overland Journal*, V (Winter, 1987), pp. 16–40.

trip Wiggins died of cholera at the Missouri River, but the widow and her children continued and established themselves at Geneva, although only a fraction of the colonists who had committed themselves ever migrated.[16]

Here in the "beautiful valley of the Neosho," as a companion would call it, Fanny Wiggins grew to young womanhood and her family was not unacquainted with adversity. Because of a scorching drought, nearly half the colonists abandoned their claims by the end of 1860. Next came hordes of grasshoppers to demolish most of the crops of 1861.[17] When Geneva was caught up in the border conflict accompanying the Civil War, it was Fanny who reportedly hid the family in the cellar.

In November, 1863, she married Josiah Shawahan Kelly, a farmer and discharged Union veteran who was at least fifteen years older than she.[18] Born in eastern Ohio, Kelly had crossed the plains to California in 1856 or 1857 where he worked in the mines for about three years, without much success.

[16] Alfred Theodore Andreas, *History of the State of Kansas* (Chicago, 1883), p. 680. See Lew Wallace Duncan and Charles F. Scott, *History of Allen and Woodson Counties*, (Iola, Kansas, 1901), p. 69; and E. Fisk, "First Settlement of Geneva, Allen County" (Geneva, Kansas, July 25, 1878), *Kansas Historical Collections*, I & II (1881).

[17] Alice Marie Miller, *The Geneva Settlement: A History* (Alva, Okla., 1972), pp. 10–11.

[18] Brown, "Attack," p. 19. The 1860 Census gives Josiah Kelly's age as thirty-three. United States Census of 1860, Allen County, Kansas, p. 24.

The Census of 1860 showed him back in Geneva, farming, with a personal estate valued at $300. Five months after their wedding, the Kellys left their home on their ill-fated western journey. Then, half a dozen years later, one of his brothers would swear that before the Kellys left Geneva, Josiah had been the owner of two "good and well improved farms" and other property in Allen County worth "at least" $8,000 or $10,000, which he had sold and started west with the proceeds. In any event, the Kellys carried with them a consignment of trade goods, including 100-pound sacks of flour, over 100 pounds of coffee and an equal weight of dried fruit, canned fruit by the case, dry goods, clothing and even kegs of alcohol, whiskey and brandy. Along with the draft animals, according to Fanny's handwritten petition in Congress, they drove a herd of fifty milk cows and twenty-five calves.[19] The total value of their merchandise and other property was given by Fanny as $15,200, quadruple her husband's estimate of two years before. All this with a party of only seven men, two women and two children.

[19] Josiah S. Kelly to Harrison Kelly (Folsom, Calif., January 29, 1859); affidavit of Harrison Kelly (Ottumwa, Kansas, March 7, 1870), House Records, 42nd Cong.; Fanny Kelly affidavit (December 24, 1870), House Committee on Indian Affairs Papers, 42nd Cong., all in Record Group 233, National Archives (copies courtesy of Randy Brown, Douglas, Wyoming). Also U. S. Census of 1860, Allen County, Kansas, p. 24; Sarah L. Larimer, *The Capture and Escape; or, Life Among the Sioux* (Philadelphia, 1870), p. 16; Senate *Report* No. 68, 41st Cong., 2nd Sess. (1869–70) [Serial 1409], p. 1.

The Kelly party included their adopted daughter, seven- or eight-year-old Mary J. Hurley (Fanny's sister's child); two Negro hands, Andy and sixteen-year-old Franklin, both of whom, it was said, had previously been slaves among the Cherokees, but had escaped after the defeat of Cherokee troops fighting for the Confederate States at the battle of Honey Creek; and Gardner Wakefield, a twenty-eight-year-old affable, likable bachelor, who was also a friend and neighbor from the Iola-Geneva area and was originally from Maine. Within a few days, they had joined forces with an elderly Methodist minister named Sharp, who was described as "blind in one eye and so cross-eyed the sight of the other was very poor" from south of Geneva; and subsequently added William J. and Sarah Luse Larimer and their seven-year-old son, Frank—acquaintances from nearby Iola who had left at the same time and had temporarily joined a larger group. Larimer was a farmer who had served briefly as a lieutenant elected in a Kansas company before receiving a medical discharge. Sarah Larimer was a photographer and hoped to practice her profession in Idaho; hence the Larimer wagons were loaded with daguerreotype equipment, chemicals and picture cases, and, if we are to believe later testimony, "a large stock of gold watches and jewelry." Along the way they picked up Noah Daniel Taylor who left his wife and eight children behind on the homestead along Wolf Creek not far from Burlington, about ten miles northwest of Geneva. He drove the four-horse team for the Larimers.[20]

In retrospect, Fanny Kelly's account indicates an optimistic, even light-hearted attitude when her long journey began. What can never be known, of course, is what went on in her own mind that she did not record. No doubt there was the typical woman's reluctance to leave an established home, friends and family, especially one's mother, but the real question concerns her feelings towards life on the trail. From past experience, she knew it would be no lark. What dark thoughts filled her mind with respect to Indian danger along the way? And when consoling little Mary's fear of Indians, was she merely whistling in the dark for the child's benefit? How familiar was she with the growing number of captivity narratives that had intrigued Americans since the days of the founding colonists? Recent research reasons that women's concerns with Indians on the trail were much more often derived from their own anxieties about what *could* happen than what actually *did* happen. A sample of 150 accounts of

[20]Larimer, *Capture and Escape*, p. 44; Irving R. Merrill, *Bound for Idaho: The 1864 Trail Journal of Julius Merrill* (Moscow, Idaho, 1988), pp. 6, 68, 174; Angie Debo, *A History of the Indians of the United States* (Norman, Okla., 1970), pp. 143-44; Kelly, *Narrative*, p. 38; Senate *Report* No. 1591, 50th Cong., 1st Sess. (1887-88) [Serial 2524]; Noah D. Taylor to his wife (in camp, near Fort Laramie, July 5, 1864); Sarah L. Larimer to Mrs. Taylor (Fort Laramie, August 15, 1864). Copies of the two letters are in the American Heritage Center, University of Wyoming.

overland travel indicates that only ten percent recorded major troubles.[21]

Yet no amount of printed or oral description of Indian atrocities could prepare the unfortunate minority when disaster struck. Presumably, Fanny Kelly had no special premonition or prior anticipation for what was about to happen to her. The prospects of a brutal assault and sudden captivity by savage tribesmen must always have been in the back of her mind, but provided no special wisdom or realistic guidelines in time of need. She had no precedents for making the agonizing decision to drop off little Mary alone in the wilderness of Wyoming, and she must have anguished when she made it and while she anxiously pondered Mary's fate, wondering if she had made the right choice. Clearly her strength of character would be sorely tested.

From a combination of Fanny's report and that of Sarah Larimer, we can trace most of the route, surmising the use of the standard trail north in Kansas, probably at first along the Neosho, then northeast along Deer and Martin Creeks, cutting northward along what later would be the line of the Santa Fe Railroad via Baldwin and Lawrence, the latter just recovering from serious damage by Quantrell's Raiders.[22] Next, the now well-established roadway

[21]Glenda Riley, "The Specter of a Savage: Rumors and Alarmism on the Overland Trail," *The Western Historical Quarterly*, XV (October, 1984), p. 433.

[22]Miller, *The Geneva Settlement*, p. 7.

was cut westward along the Kansas River, crossing by bridge west of modern Topeka, then swinging northwestward, crossing the Big Vermillion and the Big Blue rivers and angling along the Little Blue and Big Sandy Creek on to Nebraska and Fort Kearny on the Platte, a waterway described by Sarah as "beautiful," "its broad bosom dotted with islands of richest verdure, and adorned with gorgeous-hued flowers and delicate vining vegetation." Here, many westward-bound travelers were much in evidence— "the green dotted with white wagon covers, and the pasture numbering thousands of horses and cattle, resting in the lovely valley before attempting the passage of the plains and penetrating the unknown heights of the rocky peaks that rise beyond." [23]

Three miles west of the fort was Kearney City, [24] "a right promising town," one woman called it. [25] It was, according to Sarah Larimer, "a small village, built of adobe or sunburnt brick, and was then in its pristine glory." In these two dozen or so rude structures, it was said, lived "as scurvy a set of bipeds as ever demoralized a community." [26] On to the west, beyond Kearney City, or Dobytown, as it was

[23] Larimer, *Capture and Escape*, p. 18.

[24] Fort Kearny and Kearney City were named for General Stephen W. Kearny, however, Kearney City added an "e" to its official spelling in 1857. Lilian L. Fitzpatrick, *Nebraska Place-Names*, (Lincoln, Nebr., 1960) p. 25.

[25] Mary Ringo, quoted in Merrill J. Mattes, *Platte River Road Narratives* (Urbana, Ill., 1988), p. 584.

[26] Dr. C. M. Clark, quoted in Merrill J. Mattes, *The Great Platte River Road* (Lincoln, Nebr., 1969), p. 220.

called, lay a long treeless, brushless stretch, except for a few cottonwood and willows. At Cottonwood Springs, a former Pony Express station and now a military post and a growing settlement of "some magnitude," the army searched all emigrant wagons for contraband government arms and confiscated all round-barreled Colt Navy revolvers. Every ten or fifteen miles, the travelers passed "ranches," sometimes with sod or adobe houses large enough to accommodate a number of guests, especially in bad weather. Their proprietors were "generally rude specimens of humanity" concerned with providing goods and entertainment to emigrants, not with farming or grazing.[27] Fording the South Platte at the "Old California Crossing," 180 miles west of Fort Kearny, near present-day Brule, Nebraska, after a five-day delay due to high water, the highest in twenty years, the party removed the wheels and floated four wagon boxes over together, greeted at the end of the voyage by a raging thunderstorm and a further downpour of rain.[28]

Twenty miles north and west of the crossing lay Ash Hollow, site of General Harney's "indiscriminate slaughter of the rude children of nature,"[29] as a traveler expressed it later, a fact also noted less

[27]Ibid., p. 270.

[28]Merrill, *Bound for Idaho*, p. 46; Noah D. Taylor to his wife (in camp near Fort Laramie, July 5, 1864), copy, American Heritage Center.

[29]Catherine V. Waite, quoted in Mattes, *Platte River Road Narratives*, p. 544.

graphically by both Mrs. Kelly and Mrs. Larimer.

Proceeding westward, the Kelly-Larimer group passed a number of landmarks familiar to thousands of emigrants. First came Courthouse Rock, which dominated the countryside "like the remains of some old Roman castle," and on which were carved the names of a generation of pioneers.[30] Then came Chimney Rock, "the wonder of the plains," projecting into the sky like a minaret or Cleopatra's Needle, also with hundreds of names inscribed for posterity and mentioned in ninety-five percent of all trail diaries. Farther along was Scott's Bluff, described variously as "grand, sublime and magnificent," "a Nebraska Gibraltar" and "a Mausoleum which the mightiest on earth might covet."[31]

Shortly after passing these scenic spectacles, the little group had its first in-depth encounter with real Indians. Camped at Cold Creek, a stream with excellent trout fishing, they were visited by Good Horse, who had some command of English and who appeared clad in buffalo robe, moccasins, military hat, and sword. Offered supper, he refused until the food had been tasted by others, then released his horse which trotted off to his lodge a mile away, a signal for his three wives to join in the meal. After eating, Good Horse mounted his pony, which was

[30] W. S. Haskell, as quoted in Mattes, *Platte River Road Narratives*, p. 578.

[31] Quoted in Mattes, *Great Platte River Road*, pp. 422–23; Mary Elizabeth Parkhurst Warner and Mary Eliza Warner, quoted in Mattes, *Platte River Road Narratives*, p. 587.

saddled by one of his squaws, leaving his spouses to walk. He returned for breakfast and bargained arrogantly for food for his children. Even this first contact had begun to dispel some of the stereotypes carried by the newcomers. "We had read much of the noble character of the red man, of his lofty bearing, scorn, pride, etc., all of which our acquaintance with Good Horse and his family failed to confirm." [32] But other travelers of the same period were even more wary. Another woman who was also heading for Bannack just a few weeks earlier confided into her diary as she camped two days east of Fort Laramie:

> The Sioux are a numerous, intelligent, and powerful tribe. Their treachery and hostility to the white are unbounded. Their friendship is all mere pretense. All they want is an opportunity to murder the weary "pilgrim" and run off his stock. Government is now at war with them far away to the north, which, it is feared will drive them towards the Platte to commit their depredations upon the emigrants and defenseless settlers. [33]

Another twenty miles brought the wagons to Fort Laramie, one of the most historic spots in the trans-Mississippi West. Located at the foot of a gentle

[32] Larimer, *Capture and Escape*, pp. 32–34. Noah Taylor commented from near Fort Laramie that "we have not had any trouble with the Indians as yet, they appear to be very friendly. They will shake hands and say, how how now!" Noah D. Taylor to his wife (in camp near Fort Laramie, July 5, 1864), copy, American Heritage Center.

[33] S. Lyman Tyler, ed., *The Montana Gold Rush Diary of Kate Dunlap* (Salt Lake City, 1969) p. b-20.

slope at the juncture of the Laramie and North Platte rivers, with hills on three sides, Fort Laramie was a lively place, with a parade of travelers passing through and many brightly-dressed Indian wives of traders and half-breed children much in evidence—"pitiable-looking-children, of aboriginal descent, half surrounded by civilization, yet held in the lap of barbarity, smiling upon fair fathers, yet kissed by swarthy mothers."[34] Fort Laramie had "at least one hundred houses," "respectable looking" government buildings and whiskey was "much in demand by the soldiers," of whom there were between two and three hundred; but in general most emigrants were unimpressed. One young woman "saw nothing but soldiers and papooses" there. Its immediate vicinity was devoid of vegetation except for two small pines, though there were trees along the banks farther down among which were Indian burials on scaffolds. It was, as one emigrant put it during the summer of 1864, "Nothing more than a trading post with soldiers stationed there, more for ornament than use."[35]

Just beyond Fort Laramie, the trail left the river and gradually rose through hills covered with dark, short pines which gave it the name Black Hills of Wyoming, and their wild scenery made it "a fit abode for hobgoblins and ghosts," one young lady

[34]Larimer, *Capture and Escape*, p. 35.
[35]Merrill, *Bound for Idaho*, p. 57; John Rush Clark, quoted in Mattes, *Platte River Road Narratives*, p. 572.

reported.[36] Wagons now were brown-topped and dingy, having lost the shiny freshness of Geneva and Iola. Following the "bowstring cutoff" south of the North Platte, the party stopped at the Horseshoe Creek telegraph station where they received word of the quiet, peaceful nature of the country ahead. Then they wound through an attractive wooded valley, crossed La Prele Creek and eight miles farther along, planned to camp for the night beside the Little Box Elder Creek, about ten miles west of the present town of Douglas, Wyoming.[37] From there, probably the itinerary would have taken them over the standard route outlined in the popular guide, *Idaho: six months in the new gold diggings*, published in 1864 by John Lyle Campbell, a reporter for the Chicago *Tribune* who had traveled the route the year before: west along the Platte, past Independence Rock, along the Sweetwater, through South Pass, over the Lander Cutoff to Fort Hall in Idaho and on to Bannack City over a trail north from the Snake River that was "rocky as a boar's behind," according to one who had made the trip the year before.[38] But the last part

[36] Lucy Nettleton, quoted in *ibid.*, p. 563.

[37] Most of the details of the route in the previous sketch come from Larimer, *Capture and Escape*; Merrill, *Bound for Idaho*; John S. Collins, *Across the Plains in '64* (New York, 1864); Albert Jerome Dickson, *Covered Wagon Days*, (Cleveland, 1929); or other travel journals across the trail in the same year.

[38] Cicero Card, as quoted in Mattes, *Platte River Road Narratives*, p. 559.

of the journey was never completed. Little Box Elder Creek was the final stop on the trail by the ill-
fated little party of eleven with their five wagons
and small herd of stock.

Some believe that the attack on the train came as
a reaction to a grisly episode which occurred far
from the Overland Trail two weeks earlier. Captain
John Feilner, topographical engineer, was collecting
specimens with two soldiers in advance of General
Sully's main column, which paralleled the Missouri.
Near the mouth of the Little Cheyenne, Feilner was
killed by three Indians who fled. General Sully sent
the Dakota Cavalry in pursuit, killed and decapitat-
ed them, then mounted their heads on poles near
the camp as a warning. This news flew to every Indian band and electrified them. Feeling they were
about to be exterminated, the Sioux flocked to a
huge encampment between the Heart and Cannonball Rivers in Dakota.[39] Several writers theorize that
when the Oglalas met the Kelly-Larimer party early
on the day of July 12, they were friendly. Only later, having received word by messenger of the army's
atrocity on the Little Cheyenne, did they turn hostile, then swung north to help their people.[40] The

[39]Louis Pfaller, "Sully's Expedition of 1864 featuring the
Killdeer Mountain and Badlands Battles," *North Dakota
History*, XXXI (January, 1964), pp. 25-28.
[40]Doane Robinson, "The Rescue of Frances Kelly," *South
Dakota Historical Collections*, IV (1908), p. 110; Mari San-
doz, *Crazy Horse: The Strange Man of the Oglalas* (Lincoln,
Nebr., 1961 ed.), p. 147.

difficulty with this, however, is that the Indians did not make contact in the morning or even in early afternoon. The first contact came at dusk, when the train was settling in to camp. It is doubtful if Ottawa's band changed its mind after it came upon the wagons; more likely it contemplated an assault as soon as it encountered them. Considering the Indian mood in 1864, a small party of this size was the perfect temptation.

The Kansans met the Indians just after crossing Cottonwood Creek and traveled with them for an hour until instructed to halt and provide them a supper, only to be attacked without warning. With no chance to defend themselves, Sharp, Taylor and Franklin were killed at the outset. Larimer and Wakefield were both wounded; Wakefield would die eight months later at Deer Creek Station. Only Kelly and Andy escaped unscathed. After plundering the train, the Indians moved north with their captives, Mrs. Kelly and little Mary, Mrs. Larimer and her small son.

On the basis of Fanny's description, much of it no doubt gleaned from accounts and maps consulted after her release, to trace her route in captivity would be difficult, if not impossible. Crossing the Platte, the Indians moved in a general northwesterly direction to the Powder River at the site where old Fort Reno would later stand. Then they moved up the Powder and on her seventh night of captivity reached a village, presumably on the Tongue River.

By July 25th they were apparently on the northern edge of the North Dakota Bad Lands, close enough to be involved in the fight against General Sully's troops at Killdeer Mountain, two days later. Thus in thirteen days, the Indians had traveled almost 400 miles in a direct line, and no doubt longer by the circuitous route used—a remarkable feat, to say the least.[41]

Quite understandably, Fanny was unfamiliar with the terrain and includes relatively few place names in her account—those probably traced later from maps or books. Her descriptions of rivers and encampments are often so vague as to be unidentifiable. She did not know the location of the Blackfeet Sioux village, her last stop in captivity before returning to Fort Sully and freedom. In her plea for compensation from Congress in 1868, she admitted that while there she had no idea of where she was. Fanny said, "I knew there were whites somewhere on the Missouri River, but did not know my distance from any place or in what direction the Missouri was from where I was." At that particular time, she was probably a few miles west of the Missouri River in the very northern part of what was to become South Dakota, only 100 miles or so from Fort Sully, not the 200 miles she estimates in her book. In her petition to Congress, she noted that it took five days to reach Fort Sully, often through heavy snow, an impossible time schedule for anyone

[41]Robinson, "Rescue of Frances Kelly," pp. 109–10.

assuming her distance calculations were accurate.[42]

After two nights Fanny was alone in her captivity. Sarah Larimer and her son had escaped after a single night. Sarah remained silent as to how this was accomplished, but Fanny believed that she had an Indian ally. Even before that, somewhere west of Box Elder Creek on the plateau overlooking the North Platte, little Mary, as Fanny relates, was dropped off the horse and told to conceal herself until morning, then find her way back to the emigrant trail. This must have been one of the most traumatic moments of the entire ordeal for Fanny. What must have been her frame of mind once the child was gone—alone in the vast wilderness; the mother with the gnawing dread of not knowing what had happened to the little girl as well as the fate of her husband. She may have suspected the worst about Mary much earlier, probably in a few weeks, when she saw a strange Indian with "a bright and well-known shawl" and "a child's scalp of long, fair hair hanging from his saddle." It is interesting to note that this incident does not appear in the twenty-three page narrative she wrote to Congress in 1868, detailing her captivity and requesting financial support. Her petition does say that the Indians had boasted to her that they had killed little Mary and Sarah Larimer and her son. But an army

[42] *Ibid.*, p. 111; Fanny Kelly Petition (1868), Exhibit "B," House Committee on Appropriations Papers, 40th Cong., Record Group 233, National Archives.

officer at Fort Sully, two days after her ultimate release, reported that except for the fact that little Mary, Mrs. Larimer and her son had all escaped the Oglalas, Fanny Kelly "knows nothing of the fate of her companions."[43]

According to Fanny's account, Josiah Kelly and a detachment of soldiers from Deer Creek Station found little Mary's mutilated remains on July 14 and buried her in a solitary grave near where she fell. Others say that three soldiers who saw her but feared she was a decoy returned with reinforcements on July 17, found Mary dead and buried her. These troops said the road

> " ... was strewn for miles with arrows, clothing, beds, flour, bacon, salt, and other plunder; six dead men, one of them a Negro, were seen by them scattered along the road. All of them had been killed by arrows. The Indians were piling the plunder together and burning it; the wagons were not destroyed; the harness was all cut to peices [*sic*] by the Indians to get the mules out."[44]

The journal of Julius Merrill describes the finding of Mary's body on July 17, by members of the Merrill train, now combined with a much larger one as it passed near the Box Elder Creek. The body of

[43]Captain John H. Pell to General Alfred Sully (Ft. Sully, December 11, 1864), in Exhibit "C," in *ibid.* See also Frank Myers, *Soldiering in Dakota, Among the Indians, in 1863-65* (Freeport, New York, 1888, reprint 1971), p. 33.

[44]Merrill, *Bound for Idaho*, p. 174; William E. Unrau, ed., *Tending the Talking Wire: A Buck Soldier's View of Indian Country 1863-1866* (Salt Lake City, 1979), pp. 147-48.

the "harmless child" was "lying upon its face, both arms were thrown forward as if to prevent falling," and it had been shot with arrows, tomahawked and scalped by "the savage inhuman brutes." Merrill now realized why those living on the frontier had developed "so universal and deadly a hatred" against the Indians.[45]

Merrill also notes that the train left several behind to bury the remains then moved on, and Josiah Kelly subsequently wrote that others had discovered and interred Mary.[46] Perhaps Fanny credits her husband for the burial as part of her rationale and justification on his behalf. But as Merrill points out, "injured self-respect and family loyalty" cloud both of Josiah's claims and those of the three soldiers who had failed to rescue Mary.[47] After all, Josiah had fled from the attack scene without aiding his family, a fact that Fanny could rationalize since any effort to fight against the obviously overwhelming odds would only have resulted in his death.

*   *

It was during General Sully's campaign that Fanny Kelly, the Sioux Wars and the new Montana

[45] Merrill, *Bound for Idaho*, pp. 65–66.

[46] *Ibid.*, p. 66; Josiah S. Kelly to R. W. Kelly (August 15, 1864), copy courtesy of Randy Brown. The statement of another member of the emigrant train, George Foreman, agrees with Merrill. See T. A. Larson, ed., "Across the Plains in 1864 with George Foreman," *Annals of Wyoming*, XL (April, 1968), p. 20.

[47] Merrill, *Bound for Idaho*, p. 174.

gold fields all came together in the isolated corner of western Dakota. With congressional appropriations to protect emigrants on overland routes to the gold fields, Captain James Liberty Fisk conducted four overland expeditions over the northern route, three of them under auspices of the federal government and one private. The author of *Idaho: Her Gold Fields, and the Routes to Them* in 1863, Fisk was at once soldier, promoter and entrepreneur. In the summer of 1864, Fisk set out to lead a train of about a hundred wagons and some 170 Minnesotans to the Montana mines. Accompanied by fifty cavalrymen from Colonel Sibley's command, the expedition moved out from Fort Ridgley across Dakota to Fort Rice, whence his escort returned east. Fisk prevailed upon the officer in charge to furnish fifty convalescent troops to accompany the train as far as the Yellowstone, and set out following General Sully's trail up the Cannonball. After eighty miles, they turned southwestward toward the headwaters of the Little Missouri. Then on September 2, near today's town of Rhame, North Dakota, Hunkpapa Sioux warriors set upon two rear wagons of Fisk's train, killing a dozen men. During the next two days, the expedition moved twelve miles under continuing Indian attack. Now, as they neared the Montana line, an entrenched camp was set up and a courier dispatched back to Fort Rice for help. It was at this time of duress that Fanny established written contact with Fisk, but Fisk was unsuccessful in his efforts to ransom her. After several days, the Indians withdrew and in due time, September 20, the relief expedition arrived. Denied troops to escort him west, Fisk was compelled to return to Fort Rice with the expedition and Fanny's release would be delayed another two-and-a-half months.[48] Even so, her exchange of letters with Fisk dramatized her plight and prompted a hard line from the acting commandant of Fort Sully which probably speeded her rescue.

The question inevitably arises as to whether or not Fanny suffered sexual abuse by her captors, a common fate of white women who fell into Indian hands. Among the many western tribes, a white female prisoner generally became the property of the first warrior who laid hands on her. She could be sold, if he chose, but often became a drudge in his lodge and compelled to submit sexually. It was not uncommon for a rescued or ransomed victim to assert that other women had been subject to sexual mistreatment by their captors, while they themselves, for some other reasons, had been spared such abuse. Fanny comments on the lot of sixteen-year-old Mary Boyeau, a captive since the Spirit Lake uprising, whom she met while in the Sioux village and who was forced to become the second wife of a Sioux warrior. In her own situation, Fanny noted

[48]See Helen McCann White, ed., *Ho! For the Gold Fields: Northern Overland Wagon Trains of the 1860s* (St Paul, Minn., 1966), pp. 113–18.

that her captor, Ottawa, was over seventy years of age, had been wounded in a domestic quarrel and appreciated her skillful nursing, "and to this fact, doubtless, I owe my escape from a fate worse than death." Later, she commented that after the Indians had attacked the Fisk emigrant train, "while their whiskey lasted I suffered everything but death alone from their outrageous brutal treatment. Death would have been a welcome messenger at any moment." Still later, in a petition to Congress to collect compensation for her experience in the hands of the Sioux, she wrote: "Your memorialist was then taken into captivity, and was forced to become the squaw of one of the O-gal-lal-lah Chiefs, who treated her in a manner too horrible to mention, and during her captivity was passed from Chief to Chief, and treated in a similar manner."[49]

There are differences of opinion over Fanny Kelly's role in "saving" Fort Sully. It was her contention, of course, buttressed by testimonials from army officers at the post, that her advance warning, delivered by the Indian, Jumping Bear, prevented her Blackfeet escort from taking over the fort. These Indians, she believed, planned to attack the garrison by using her as a decoy. Subsequently, Fanny made a strong case for herself and ultimately

[49] Fanny Kelly Petition (1868), Exhibit "B," House Committee on Appropriations, 40th Cong. Record Group 233, National Archives; Fanny Kelly Memorial, *To the Senators and Members of the House of Representatives of Congress* (no date), Newberry Library, Chicago. See Appendix pp. 335–37.

Congress acknowledged her contribution in saving the fort with compensation of $5,000.[50] But another theory is that Fort Sully was never in any danger. Historian Doane Robinson (who refers to her as Frances Kelly) argues that a small group of Blackfeet led by Crawler were actually Fanny's deliverers and the larger band who helped escort her to the fort had no hostile intentions whatever, but went mainly for the feast they knew they would be given as a result.[51] Although earlier rejected as a figment of an old Indian's imagination, this story does have merit. Evidence does seem to indicate that once Fanny's whereabouts was ascertained (a conclusion from her exchange of correspondence with Captain James Fisk at the time of the attack on his wagon train) the army took a hard-nosed stance with the Blackfeet Sioux, who were by this time more than ready for peace talks. At Fort Sully, Major Albert E. House of the Sixth Iowa Cavalry, on express instructions from his superior officer, had sent several Blackfeet with specific instructions to obtain Fanny Kelly's release as a precondition for peace. With drawn knives, they had been successful in freeing her by force. Fanny's own 1868 petition to Congress bears this out, although her book itself is remarkably vague on how she came into the hands of the Blackfeet Sioux party which escorted her to freedom. Contemporary accounts make no mention of

---

[50] 16 *United States Statutes at Large*, Private Acts, p. 32.
[51] Robinson, "Rescue of Frances Kelly," pp. 114–15, 117.

fear of attack at the time of her delivery. Only later did several of the men and officers of the Iowa Sixth Cavalry back up her claim with affidavits. But Major House denied that she had "saved" the fort. "It was my duty at all times to be prepared for an attack by hostile Indians and I was so prepared," he testified.[52] Fanny, however, convinced Washington. In 1870, Congress voted her $5,000 for her efforts in warning Captain Fisk and Fort Sully, and two years later authorized an additional $10,000 for full payment of property taken and destroyed by the Sioux when the Kelly wagons were attacked.[53]

*　　　*

Today in a parking area off Interstate 25, west of the Natural Bridge Road exit, a stone memorial, erected by the Historic Landmark Commission of Wyoming, reads as follows:

Three men named Sharp, Franklin, and Taylor,
and one unknown man
were killed by Indians July 12, 1864
where the Oregon Trail crosses Little Box
Elder Creek 2½ miles S. W. of here.
They are buried 4 miles S. W. by the grave of
Mary Kelly who also was killed July 13, 1864.

[52]Brown, "Attack," pp. 32-33; Leavenworth, Kansas, *The Daily Times*, December 13, 1864; Albert E. House deposition (Delhi, Iowa, June 26, 1876), in Fanny Kelly *vs.* Sarah L. Larimer, *et al.*, microfilm of Case File 1780, Franklin County District Court, Kansas Historical Society.
[53]16 *United States Statutes at Large*, Private Acts, p. 32; 17 *United States Statutes at Large*, Private Acts, pp. 37-38.

Fanny Kelly is buried 2,000 miles away in the nation's capital, but her most enduring monument is her book, *Narrative of My Captivity among the Sioux Indians*, an account which is still compelling and fascinating reading.

CLARK C. SPENCE
MARY LEE SPENCE

University of Illinois, Champaign-Urbana
April, 1990

Narrative of My Captivity
among the Sioux Indians

I

"Ho! for Idaho"

I WAS born in Orillia, Canada, in 1845.[1] Our home was on the lake shore, and there amid pleasant surroundings I passed those happy days of my early childhood.

The years 1852 to 1856 witnessed, probably, the heaviest immigration the West has ever known in a corresponding length of time. Those who had gone before sent back to their friends such marvelous accounts of the rapid development of the country, the fertility of the soil, and the ease with which fortunes were made, the "Western fever" became almost epidemic. Whole towns in the old, Eastern States were almost depopulated. Old substantial farmers, surrounded apparently by all the comforts that heart could wish, sacrificed the homes wherein their families had been reared for generations, and, with all their worldly possessions, turned their faces toward the setting sun. And with what high hopes! Alas! how few, comparatively, met their realization.

In 1856, my father, James Wiggins, joined a New York colony bound for Kansas. Being favorably impressed with the country and its people, he located

[1] Fanny's tombstone in Glenwood Cemetery, Washington, D.C., gives the date of her birth as November 15, 1842.

in the town of Geneva, and my father returned for his family.

Upon reaching the Missouri River on the way to our new home, my father was attacked with cholera, and died.

In obedience to his dying instructions, my widowed mother, with her little family, continued on the way to our new home. But, oh! with what saddened hearts we entered into its possession. It seemed as if the light of our life had gone out. He who had been before to prepare that home for us, was not there to share it with us, and, far away from all early associations, almost alone in a new and sparsely settled country, it seemed as though hope had died.

But God is merciful. He prepares the soul for its burdens. Of a truth, "He tempers the wind to the shorn lamb."

Our family remained in this pleasant prairie home, where I was married to Josiah S. Kelly.

My husband's health failing, he resolved upon a change of climate. Accordingly, on the seventeenth of May, 1864, a party of six persons, consisting of Mr. Gardner Wakefield, my husband, myself, our adopted daughter (my sister's child), and two Negro servants, started from Geneva, with high-wrought hopes and pleasant anticipations of a romantic and delightful journey across the plains, and a confident expectation of future prosperity among the golden hills of Idaho.

A few days after commencing our journey, we were joined by Mr. Sharp, a Methodist clergyman, from Verdigris River, about thirty miles south of Geneva; and, a few weeks later, we overtook a large train of emigrants, among whom were a family from Allen County with whom we were acquainted—Mr. Larimer, wife, and child, a boy eight years old. Preferring to travel with our small train, they left the larger one and became members of our party. The addition of one of my own sex to our little company was cause of much rejoicing to me, and helped relieve the dullness of our tiresome march.

The hours of noon and evening rest were spent in preparing our frugal meals, gathering flowers with our children, picking berries, hunting curiosities, or gazing in rapt wonder and admiration at the beauties of this strange, bewildering country.

Our amusements were varied. Singing, writing to friends at home, reading, or pleasant conversation, occupied our leisure hours.

So passed the first few happy days of our emigration to the land of sunshine and flowers.

As the sun was setting, and its last rays were flecking the towering peaks of the Rocky Mountains, gathering around the campfires, in our homelike tent, we ate with a relish known only to those who, like us, scented the pure air, and lived as nature demanded.

At night, our camp was always arranged by Andy and Franklin, our Negro men, and it was always in the same relative position. Mr. Kelly, who rode a few miles ahead as evening drew near, selected the camping ground.

The atmosphere, which during the day was hot and stifling, became cool, and was laden with the odor of prairie flowers, the night dews filling their beautiful cups with the waters of heaven.

The solemnity of the night pervaded everything. The warblings of the feathered tribes had ceased. The antelope and deer rested on the hills; no sound of laughing, noisy children, as in a settled country; no tramping of busy feet, or hurrying to and fro. All is silent. Nature, like man, has placed aside the labors of the day, and is enjoying rest and peace.

Yonder, as a tiny spark, a far-distant star might be seen from the road; a little campfire in the darkness spread over the earth.

Every eye in our little company is closed, every hand still, as we lay in our snugly-covered wagons, awaiting the dawn of another day.

And the Eye that never sleeps watched over us in our lonely camp, and cared for all the slumbering travelers.

Mr. Wakefield, with whom we became acquainted after he came to settle at Geneva, proved a most agreeable companion. Affable and courteous, unselfish, and a gentleman, we remember him with profound respect.

A fine bridge crosses the Kansas River. A half-hour's ride through the dense heavy timber, over a jet-black soil of incalculable richness, brought us to this bridge, which we crossed.

We then beheld the lovely valley of the prairies, intersecting the deepened green of graceful slopes, where waves tall prairie grass, among which the wild flowers grow.

Over hundreds of acres these blossoms are scattered, yellow, purple, white, and blue, making the earth look like a rich carpet of variegated colors; those blooming in spring are of tender, modest hue, while those of later summer and early autumn are clothed in gorgeous splendor. Solomon's gold and purple could not outrival them.

Nature seemingly reveled in beauty, for beauty's sake alone, for none but the simple children of the forest to view her in state.

Slowly the myriad years come and go upon her solitary places. Tender springtime and glorious summer drop down their gifts from overflowing coffers, while the steps of bounding deer or the notes of singing birds break upon the lonely air.

The sky is of wonderful clearness and transparency. Narrow belts and fringes of forest mark the way of winding streams.

In the distance rise conical mounds wrapped in the soft veil of dim and dreamy haze.

Upon the beaten trail are emigrants wending their way, their household goods packed in long covered wagons drawn by oxen, mules, or horses; speculators working their way to some new town with women and children; and we meet with half-breed girls, with long, heavy eyelashes and sun-burnt cheeks, jogging along on horseback.

I was surprised to see so many women among the emigrants, and to see how easily they adapted themselves to the hardships experienced in a journey across the plains.

As a rule, the emigrants traveled without tents, sleeping in and under wagons, without removing their clothing.

Cooking among emigrants to the Far West is a very primitive operation, a frying pan and perhaps a Dutch oven comprising the major part of the kitchen furniture.

The scarcity of timber is a source of great inconvenience and discomfort, "buffalo chips" being the substitute. At some of the stations, where opportunity offered, Mr. Kelly bought wood by the pound, as I had not yet been long enough inured to plains privations to relish food cooked over a fire made with "chips" of that kind.

We crossed the Platte River by binding four wagon boxes together, then loaded the boat with goods, and were rowed across by about twenty men.

We were several days in crossing. Our cattle and horses swam across. The air had been heavy and oppressively hot; now the sky began to darken suddenly, and just as we reached the opposite shore, a gleam of lightning, like a forked tongue of flame, shot out of the black clouds, blinding us by its flash, and was followed by a frightful crash of thunder.

Another gleam and another crash followed, and the dense blackness lowered threateningly over us, almost shutting out the heights beyond, and seeming to encircle us like prisoners in the valley that lay at our feet.

The vivid flashes, lighting the darkness for an instant, only made its gloom more fearful, and the heavy rolling of the thunder seemed almost to rend the heavens above it.

All at once it burst upon our unprotected heads in rain. But such rain! Not the gentle droppings of an afternoon shower, nor a commonplace storm, but a sweeping avalanche of water, drenching us completely at the first dash, and continuing to pour, seeming to threaten the earth on which we stood, and tempt the old Platte to rise and claim us as its very own.

Our wagon covers had been removed in the fording, and we had no time to put up tents for our protection until its fury was exhausted. And so we were forced to brave the elements, with part of our company on the other side of the swollen river, and a wild scene, we could scarcely discern through the pelting rain, surrounding us.

One soon becomes heroic in an open-air life, and so we put up what shelter we could when the abating storm gave us opportunity; and, wringing the water out of our clothes, hair, and eyebrows, we camped in cheerful hope of a bright tomorrow, which did not disappoint us, and our hundreds of emigrant companions scattered on the way.

Each recurring Sabbath was gratefully hailed as a season of thought and repose; as a matter of conscience and duty we observed the day, and took pleasure in doing so.

We had divine service performed, observing the ceremonies of prayer, preaching, and singing, which was fully appreciated in our absence from home and its religious privileges.

Twenty-five miles from California Crossing is a place called Ash Hollow, where the eye is lost in space as it endeavors to penetrate its depths. Here some years before, General Harney made his name famous by an indiscriminate massacre of a band of hostile Indians with their women and children.

II

The Attack and the Capture

A TRAIN of wagons was wending its westward way
with visions of the future bright as our own.
Sometimes a single team might be seen traveling
alone. Our party was among the many small squads
emigrating to the land of promise.

The day on which our doomed family was scattered and killed was the twelfth of July, a warm and
oppressive day. The burning sun poured forth its
hottest rays upon the great Black Hills and the vast
plains of Montana, and the great emigrant road was
strewed with men, women, and children, and flocks
of cattle, representing towns of adventurers.

We looked anxiously forward to the approach of
evening, with a sense of relief, after the excessive
heat of the day.

Our journey had been pleasant, but toilsome, for
we had been long weeks on the road.

Slowly our wagons wound through the timber
that skirted the Little Box Elder, and, crossing the
stream, we ascended the opposite bank.

We had no thought of danger or timid misgivings
on the subject of savages, for our fears had been all
dispersed by constantly received assurances of their
friendliness.

11

At the outposts and ranches, we heard nothing but ridicule of their pretensions to warfare, and at Fort Laramie, where information that should have been reliable was given us, we had renewed assurances of the safety of the road and friendliness of the Indians.

At Horseshoe Creek, which we had just left, and where there was a telegraph station, our inquiries had elicited similar assurances as to the quiet and peaceful condition of the country through which we must pass.

Being thus persuaded that fears were groundless, we entertained none, and, as I have mentioned before, our small company preferred to travel alone on account of the greater progress we were able to make in that manner.

The beauty of the sunset and the scenery around us filled our hearts with joy, and Mr. Wakefield's voice was heard in song for the last time as he sang, "Ho! for Idaho." Little Mary's low, sweet voice, too, joined in the chorus. She was so happy in her childish glee on that day, as she always was. She was the star and joy of our whole party.

We wended our way peacefully and cheerfully on, without a thought of the danger that was lying like a tiger in ambush in our path.

Without a sound of preparation or a word of warning, the bluffs before us were covered with a party of about two hundred and fifty Indians, painted and equipped for war, who soon uttered a wild

war whoop and fired a signal volley of guns and revolvers into the air.

This terrible and unexpected apparition came
upon us with such startling swiftness that we had
not time to think before the main body halted and
sent out a part of their force, which circled us round
at regular intervals, but some distance from our
wagons. Recovering from the shock, our men instantly resolved on defense, and corralled the wagons. My husband was looked upon as leader, as he
was principal owner of the train. Without regard to
the insignificance of our numbers, Mr. Kelly was
ready to stand his ground; but, with all the power I
could command, I entreated him to forbear and
only attempt conciliation. "If you fire one shot," I
said, "I feel sure you will seal our fate, as they seem
to outnumber us ten to one, and will at once massacre all of us."

Love for the trembling little girl at my side, my
husband, and friends, made me strong to protest
against anything that would lessen our chance for
escape with our lives. Poor little Mary! From the first
she had entertained an ungovernable dread of the
Indians, a repugnance that could not be overcome,
although in our dealings with friendly savages, I had
endeavored to show how unfounded it was, and
persuade her that they were civil and harmless, but
all in vain. Mr. Kelly bought her beads and many
little presents from them which she much admired,
but she would always add, "They look so cross at

me and they have knives and tomahawks, and I fear they will kill me." Could it be that her childish young mind had some presentiment or warning of her horrid fate?

My husband advanced to meet the chief and demand his intentions.

The savage leader immediately came toward him uttering the friendly words, "How! How!"

His name was Ottawa, and he was a war chief of the Oglala band of the Sioux nation.[1] He at once struck himself on his breast, saying, "Good Indian, me," and while pointing to those around him, he continued, "Heap good Indian, hunt buffalo and deer." He assured us of his utmost friendship for all white people. He shook hands while others crowded around our wagons, shaking us all by the hand over and over again, until our arms ached, and grinning and nodding with demonstrations of goodwill.

Our only policy seemed to be temporizing, in hope of assistance approaching; and, to gain time, we allowed them unopposed to do whatever they fancied. First, they said they would like to change one of their horses for the one Mr. Kelly was riding, a favorite racehorse. Very much against his will, he acceded to their request, and gave up to them the noble animal to which he was fondly attached.

My husband came to me with words of cheer and

[1] Historians have not been able to identify Ottawa or Silver Horn, as he was also called, with any known Oglala chief.

hope, but oh! what a marked look of despair was upon his face, such as I had never seen before.

The Indians asked for flour, and we gave them what they wanted of provisions. Then they emptied all of it upon the ground, saving only the sack. They talked to us partly by signs and partly in broken English, with which some of them were quite familiar, and as we were anxious to suit ourselves to their whims and preserve a friendly situation as long as possible, we allowed them to take whatever they desired, and offered them many presents besides. It was, as I have said before, extremely warm weather, but they remarked that the cold made it necessary for them to look for clothing, and begged for some from our stock, which was granted without the slightest offered objection on our part. I, in a careless-like manner, said they must give me some moccasins for some articles of clothing that I had just handed them, and a very pleasant young Indian gave me a nice pair, richly embroidered with different colored beads.

Our anxiety to conciliate them increased every moment, for the hope of help arriving from some quarter grew stronger as they dallied, and, alas! it was our only one.

They grew bolder and more insolent in their advances. One of them laid hold of my husband's gun, but, being repulsed, desisted.

The chief at last intimated that he desired us to proceed on our way, promising that we should not be molested. We obeyed, without trusting them, and soon the train was again in motion, the Indians insisting on driving our herd, and growing ominously familiar. Soon my husband called a halt. He noted that we were approaching a rocky glen, in whose gloomy depths he anticipated a murderous attack, and from which escape would be utterly impossible. Our enemies urged us still forward, but we resolutely refused to stir, when they requested that we should prepare supper, which they said they would share with us, and then go to the hills to sleep. The men of our party concluded it best to give them a feast and Mr. Kelly gave orders to our two servants to prepare a large meal immediately for the Indians.

Andy said, "I think, if I know anything about it, they had their supper," since they had been eating sugar crackers from our wagons for some time.

The two black men had been slaves among the Cherokees, and knew the Indian character by experience. Their fear and horror of them was unbounded, and their terror seemed pitiable to us, as they had worked for us a long time, and were most faithful, trustworthy servants.

Each man was helping to prepare the supper; Mr. Larimer and Frank were getting a fire started; Mr. Wakefield was sorting out provisions from the wagon; Mr. Taylor was feeding his team; Mr. Kelly and Andy were at a distance gathering wood; Mr. Sharp was distributing sugar among the Indians.

Supper, that they asked for, was in rapid progress of preparation, when suddenly our terrible enemies threw off their masks and displayed their truly demoniac character. There was a simultaneous discharge of arms, and when the cloud of smoke cleared away, I could see the retreating form of Mr. Larimer and also the faltering motions of poor Mr. Wakefield, for he was mortally wounded.

Mr. Kelly and Andy made a miraculous escape with their lives. Mr. Sharp was killed within a few feet of me. Mr. Taylor—I never can forget his face as I saw him shot through the forehead with a rifle ball. He looked at me as he fell backward to the ground, a corpse. I was the last object that met his dying gaze. Our poor, faithful Frank fell at my feet pierced by many arrows. I recall the scene with a sickening horror. I could not see my husband anywhere, and did not know his fate, but feared and trembled. With a glance at my surroundings, my senses seemed gone for a time, but I could only live and endure.

I had but little time for thought, for the Indians quickly sprang into our wagons, tearing off covers, breaking, crushing, and smashing all hinderances to plunder, breaking open locks, trunks, and boxes, and distributing or destroying our goods with great rapidity, using their tomahawks to pry open boxes, which they split up in savage recklessness.

Oh, what horrible sights met my view! The pen is powerless to portray the scenes occurring around me. They filled the air with the fearful war whoops and hideous shouts. I endeavored to keep my fears as quiet as possible, knowing that an indiscreet act on my part might result in jeopardizing our lives, though I felt certain that we two helpless women would share death by their hands; but with as much of an air of indifference as I could command, I kept still, hoping to prolong our lives, even if but a few moments. I was not allowed this quiet but a moment, when two of the most savage-looking of the party rushed up into my wagon with tomahawks drawn in their right hands, and with their left seized me by both hands and pulled me violently to the ground, injuring my limbs very severely, almost breaking them, from the effects of which I afterward suffered a great deal. I turned to my little Mary, who, with outstretched hands, was standing in the wagon, took her in my arms and helped her to the ground. I then turned to the chief, put my hand upon his arm, and implored his protection for my fellow-prisoner and our children. At first he gave me no hope, but seemed utterly indifferent to my prayers. Partly in words and partly by signs, he ordered me to remain quiet, placing his hand upon his revolver, that hung in a belt at his side, as an argument to enforce obedience.

A short distance in the rear of our train a wagon was in sight. The chief immediately dispatched a detachment of his band to capture or to cut it off from us, and I saw them ride furiously off in pursuit

"The Attack and Capture of Our Train, July 12, 1864"
(From the First Edition)

Courtesy Newberry Library

of the small party, which consisted only of one family and a man who rode in advance of the single wagon. The horseman was almost instantly surrounded and killed by a volley of arrows. The husband of the family quickly turned his team around and started them at full speed, gave the whip and lines to his wife, who held close in her arms her youngest child. He then went to the back end of his wagon and threw out boxes, trunks, everything that he possessed. His wife meantime gave all her mind and strength to urging the horses forward on their flight from death. The Indians had by this time come very near, so that they riddled the wagon cover with bullets and arrows, one passing through the sleeve of the child's dress in its mother's arms, but doing it no personal injury.

The terrified man kept the Indians at bay with his revolver, and finally they left him and rode furiously back to the scene of the murder of our train.

III

My Husband's Agony

WHEN the Indians fired their fatal volley into
the midst of our little company, while we
were fast preparing to entertain them with a hos-
pitable supper, my husband was some distance from
the scene of horror; but, startled by the unexpected
report, he hurriedly glanced around, saw the pale,
terror-stricken faces of his wife and child, and the
Reverend Mr. Sharp's fall from the wagon, while
in the act of reaching for sugar and other articles of
food with which to conciliate our savage guests.
The hopelessness of the situation struck a chill to
his heart. Having laid down his gun to assist in the
preparation of the feast, the complete futility of
contending single-handed against such a host of infuriated demons was too apparent. His only hope,
and that a slight one indeed, was that the Indians
might spare the lives of his wife and child to obtain
a ransom. In this hope he resolved upon efforts for
the preservation of his own life that he might afterward put forth efforts for our rescue, either by pursuit and strategy, or by purchase.

He was shot at, and the barbed arrows whizzed
past him, some passing through his clothing. He saw
Mr. Wakefield fall, and knew that he was wounded,

21

if not killed. Mr. Larimer passed him in his flight for life toward some neighboring timber.

Mr. Kelly then ran for some tall grass and sage-brush, where he could conceal himself, favored by the fast approaching darkness. Scarcely daring to breathe, his mind tortured with agonizing fears for the fate of his wife and child, he seemed to hear from them the cry for help, and at one time re-solved to rush to their rescue, or die with them; any fate seemed better than such torturing doubt. But, realizing at last the utter hopelessness of an attempt at rescue, and knowing that it was a custom of the Indians, on occasion, to spare the lives of white women and children taken captive for ransom, he again resolved, if possible, to save his own life so that he might devote all his energies, and the rem-nant of fortune the savages had not despoiled him of, to the accomplishment of the rescue of his wife and child.

Lying in his perilous shelter, he saw darkness creep slowly around the hills, closing on the scene of murder and devastation, like a curtain of mercy dropped to shut out a hideous sight. He heard the noise from breaking and crashing boxes, and the voices of the Indians calling to each other; then came the culmination of his awful suspense. The Indians had again mounted their horses, and, rais-ing the terrible war song, chanted its ominous notes as they made their way across the hills, carrying his yearning thoughts with them. The pen is powerless to portray his agony during those fearful moments.

Still fearing to move in the darkness, he distinguished footsteps close to him, and knew by the stealthy tread that they were those of an Indian. In breathless silence he crouched close to the ground, fearing each instant the descent of the tomahawk and the gleam of the scalping knife, when, strange to say, a venomous reptile came to his rescue, and his enemy fled before it. A huge rattlesnake, one of the many with which that region is infested, raised its curved neck close beside him, and, thrusting forth its poisonous fangs, gave a warning rattle. The prowling Indian took alarm at the sound; other snakes, roused for the safety of their young in the dens around, repeated it, and the savage, knowing it would be death to venture further, retreated, leaving my husband where he had taken refuge; for, although he must have lain close to the noisome reptile, he was not harmed, and the greater horror of his human foe rendered him almost indifferent to the dangers of his surroundings.

Cautiously he crawled out of the weeds and grass, and, slowly rising to his feet, started swiftly in an eastward direction. He had to go far out into the hills to avoid the savages, and, after traveling many miles around, he, at last, reached the large wagon train that had been following us.

They had already been consolidating with other trains for defense, and would not venture to join Mr. Kelly, although he earnestly implored assistance to go out in aid of his friends and family, if any of them should be left alive.

The black man, Andy, soon after joined them. He came in running and in great excitement, and was about to report all the company killed, when he joyfully discovered Mr. Kelly.

Great consternation and alarm had spread with the tidings of the massacre, and fears for personal safety prevented anyone from joining my unhappy husband in an effort to rescue his wife and child or succor his missing companions.

The train did not move forward until reenforced by many others along the road; and even then every precaution was taken to secure safety and prevent a surprise. Women in several instances drove the teams, to prevent their husbands or fathers being taken at a disadvantage; weapons were being held in every man's hands, and vigilant eyes were fixed on every bluff or gorge anticipating attack.

A little time and travel brought them to the first scene of murder where they found the dead body of the companion of the man who so narrowly escaped with his family. They placed the body in a wagon, and proceeded onto the dreaded spot where the slaughter of our party had occurred.

The wagons still were standing, and feathers, flour, the remnants of much that was but half destroyed, lay scattered about the ground.

Mr. Kelly, with faltering steps, supported by the strong arm of Andy, was among the first to search the spot; his intense distress for the unknown fate of his family urged him on, although he dreaded the thought of what that bloody spot might disclose to him.

The dead bodies of Mr. Sharp, Mr. Taylor, and Franklin, were discovered lying where they had fallen. Poor Frank had been shot by an arrow that pierced both his legs, pinning them together, in which condition he had been murdered by the ruthless wretches by having his skull broken.

Both Mr. Sharp and Mr. Taylor left large families at home to mourn their loss. Mr. Larimer came up with an arrow wound in one of his limbs. He had passed the night in trying to elude his savage pursuers, and was very tired and exhausted, and very much distressed about his wife and son, a robust little fellow of eight or nine years.

But Mr. Wakefield was nowhere to be seen. After searching the brushwood for some time, and a quarter of a mile distant from the scene of attack, they discovered him still alive, but pierced by three arrows that he had vainly endeavored to extract, succeeding only in withdrawing the shafts, but leaving the steel points still deeply imbedded in the flesh. Mr. Kelly took him and cared for him with all the skill and kindness possible. No brothers could have been more tenderly attached to each other than they. He then procured as comfortable a conveyance as he could for them, and picked up a few relics from our demolished train. Among them was a daily journal I had kept from the time we were married until the hour that the Indians came upon us.

After the wounded were tended, the dead were buried. A wide grave was dug and the four bodies solemnly consigned, uncoffined, to the earth. A buffalo robe was placed over them, and then the earth was piled on their unconscious breasts.

At that time, the question of color had occasioned much dissension, and feelings were mixed as to the propriety of allowing black people the privilege of sitting beside their white brethren.[1] Poor Franklin had shared death with our companions, and was not deemed unworthy to share the common grave of his fellow victims. They lie together in the valley of Little Box Elder, where with saddened hearts our friends left them, thinking of the high hopes and fearless energy with which they had started on their journey, each feeling secure in the success that awaited them, and never, for a moment, dreaming of the grave in the wilderness that was to close over them and their earthly hopes. They were buried on a desolate plain, a thousand miles away from their loved ones, who bemoan their sad, untimely fate.

Mr. Kelly found part of his herd of cattle grazing nearby, and Mr. Sharp's were still tied to the stake where he had carefully secured them. The Indians had taken our horses, but left the cattle, as they do when they are on the warpath, or unless they need

[1] The reader is reminded that in 1864 this kind of deprecatory thinking permeated much of American society.

meat for immediate use. They shot some of them, however, and left them to decay upon the plain. Many arrows were scattered upon the ground, their peculiar marks showing that their owners had all belonged to one tribe, though of different bands. They were similar in form and finish; the shafts were round and three feet long, grooved on their sides so that the blood of the victim might not be impeded in its outward flow; each had three strips of feathers attached to its top, about seven inches in length, and, on the other end, a steel point, fastened lightly, so as to be easily detached in the flesh it penetrates. The depth of the wound depends on the distance of the aim, but they sometimes pass completely through the body, though usually their force is exhausted in entering a few inches beyond the point.

After the wounded were made as comfortable as circumstances would allow, the train left the spot in the evening and moved forward to an encampment a mile distant from the sad place, where the journey of our lost friends had ended forever, and whose visions of the golden land must be brighter and higher than earthly eyes can claim.

Early next day the travelers arrived at Deer Creek Fort,[2] where Mr. Kelly found medical aid for the

[2]Situated just east of present Glenrock, Wyoming, Deer Creek Station had served as a Pony Express and stagecoach stop before it became a telegraph station in 1861 and a camp for a limited number of troops during the Sioux problems.

wounded and procured a tent to shelter them, then devoted himself to alleviating their sufferings, and with the assistance of the kind people of the fort, succeeded in arranging them in tolerable comfort.

Captain Rhineheart[3] was commanding officer at Deer Creek, and ordered Mr. Kelly to turn over to him the property of the deceased.

The story of the attack and massacre had traveled faster than the sufferers from its barbarity. The garrison had learned it before the train arrived through some soldiers returning from Fort Laramie, where they had been to receive money from the paymaster, who had heard an account of the attack on the road, and had a passing glimpse of the terrible field of slaughter.

The same evening that the large train arrived at the fort, the officers gave a ball, and the emigrant women from the trains in the vicinity were invited to join in this inappropriately timed festivity.

The mother of the child, who had so narrowly escaped death, having lost her own wardrobe in her efforts to escape from charging Indians, borrowed a dress from a lady who resided at the fort, and attended the entertainment, dancing and joining in the gayeties, when the burial of their companion and our poor men had just been completed, and the

[3]Captain Levi M. Rinehart of Company G, Eleventh Ohio Volunteer Cavalry, enlisted in Columbus in 1863 but proved an inept commander. Court-martialed for drunkenness and neglect of duty, he was killed late in 1864 by the Sioux before the proceedings were completed.

heavy cloud of our calamity had so lately shrouded them in gloom. Such are the effects of isolation from social and civil influence, and contact with danger, and familiarity with terror and death.

People grow reckless, and often lose the gentle sympathies that alleviate suffering from frequent contact with it in its worst forms.

IV

The Beginning of My Captivity

THE FACTS related in the preceding chapter concerning matters occurring in Mr. Kelly's experience and adventures after the attack upon our train were provided to me by my husband after my restoration to freedom.

I now return to the narration of my own terrible experiences.

I was led a short distance from the wagon with Mary, and told to remain quiet, and tried to submit; but oh! what a yearning sprang up in my heart to escape, as I hoped my husband had done! But many watchful eyes were upon me, and with enemies on every side, I realized that any effort then at escape would result in failure and probably bring about the death of all the prisoners.

Mrs. Larimer, with her boy, came to us trembling with fear, saying, "The men have all escaped, and left us to the mercy of the savages."

In reply I said, "I do hope they have. What benefit would it be to us to have them here, to suffer this fear and danger with us? They would be killed, and then all hope of rescue for us would be at an end."

Her agitation was extreme. Her grief seemed to have reached its climax when she saw the Indians

destroying her property, which consisted principal-
ly of such articles as belong to the Daguerrean art.
She had indulged in high hopes of fortune from the
prosecution of this art among the mining towns of
Idaho. As she saw her chemicals, picture cases, and
other property pertaining to her calling being destroyed, she uttered a wild, despairing cry which
brought the chief of the band to us, and who, with
gleaming knife, threatened to end all her further
troubles in this world. The moment was a critical
one for her. The Indians were flushed with an easy-
won victory over a weak party; they had "tasted
blood," and it needed but slight provocation for
them to shed that even of defenseless women and
children.

My own agony could be no less than that of my
companion in misfortune. The loss of our worldly
possessions, which were not inconsiderable, consisting of a large herd of cattle, and groceries, and
goods of particular value in the mining regions, I
gave no thought to. The possible fate of my husband; the dark, fearful future that loomed before
myself and little Mary, for whose possible future I
had more apprehension than for my own, were
thoughts that flashed through my mind to the exclu-
sion of all mere pecuniary considerations.

But my poor companion was in great danger, and
perhaps it was a selfish thought of future loneliness
in captivity which induced me to intercede that her
life might be spared. I went to the side of the chief,

and, assuming a cheerfulness I was very far from feeling, pleaded successfully for her life.

I endeavored in every way to propitiate our savage captor, but received no evidences of kindness or relenting that I could then understand. He did present me, however, a wreath of gay feathers from his own head, which I took, regarding it merely as an ornament, when in reality, as I afterward learned, it was a token of his favor and protection.

He then left us to secure his own share of plunder, but we saw that we were surrounded by a special guard of armed men, and so gave up all struggle against what seemed an inevitable doom, and sat down upon the ground in despair.

I know now that night had come upon us while we sat there, and that darkness was closing the scene of desolation and death before their arrangements for departure were completed.

The first intimation we had that our immediate massacre was not intended was a few articles of clothing presented by a young Indian, whose name was Wechela, who intimated that we would have need for them.

It was a pitiable sight to see the terrified looks of our helpless children, who clung to us for the protection we could not give. Mrs. Larimer was unconscious of the death of any of our party. I did not tell her what my eyes had beheld because I feared that she simply could not endure it, but I strove to encourage and enliven her, lest her excitement would

Sarah L. Larimer

Courtesy American Heritage Center,
University of Wyoming

hasten her death or excite the anger of our captors.

We both feared that when the Indians made their arrangements for departure, we would be quickly disposed of by the scalping knife; or even should we escape for the time, we saw no prospect of release from bondage. Terror of the most appalling nature for the fate of the children possessed me, and all the horrors of Indian captivity that we had ever heard crowded on our minds with a new and fearful meaning—the slow fires, the pitiless knife, the poisoned arrows, the torture of famine, and a thousand nameless phantoms of agony passed before our troubled souls filling us with fears so harrowing that the pangs of dissolution compared to them must have been relief.

It may be thought almost impossible in such a chaos of dread to collect the soul in prayer, but

> *When woe is come, the soul is dumb*
> *That crieth not to God,*

and the only respite we could claim from despair was the lifting of our trembling hearts upward to the God of mercy.

Those hours of misery can never be forgotten. We were oppressed by terrors we could not explain or realize. The sudden separation from those we loved and relied on; our own helplessness and the gloom of uncertainty that hung over the future— surely none can better testify to the worth of trust in God than those whose hope on earth seemed ended; and, faint and weak as our faith was, it saved us from utter desolation and the complete blackness of despair.

From among the confused mass of many kinds of material scattered about, the same young Indian, Wechela, brought me a pair of shoes; also a pair of little Mary's. He looked kindly as he laid these articles before me, intimating by his gestures that our lives were to be spared, and that we should have need for them and other clothing during our long march into captivity. He also brought me some books and letters, all of which I thankfully received. I readily conceived a plan to make good use of them, and secreted as many as I could about my clothing. I said to Mrs. Larimer, "If I can retain these papers and letters and we are forced to travel with the Indians into their unknown country, I shall drop them at intervals along the way we are taken as a guide, and trust in God that our friends may find and follow them to our rescue, or if an opportunity of escape occurs, we will seize it, and by their help retrace our steps."

The property that the Indians could not carry with them, they gathered into a pile and lighted. The light of the flames showed us the forms of our captors busily loading their horses and ours with plunder, and preparing to depart. When their arrangements were completed, they came to us and signified that we must accompany them, pointing to the horses they led up to us and motioning for us to mount. The horse assigned to me was one that had belonged to Mr. Larimer and was crippled in the back. This I endeavored to make them understand, but failed.

This was the first reliable assurance they gave us that our lives were not in immediate danger, and we received it gratefully, for with the prospect of life, hope revived, and faith to believe that God had not forsaken us and that we might yet be united to our friends, who never seemed dearer than when we were about to be carried into captivity by the hostile sons of the forest.

Many persons have since assured me that, to them, death would have been preferable to life with such prospects, saying that rather than have submitted to be carried away by savages to a dark and doubtful doom, they would have taken their own lives. But it is only those who have looked over the dark abyss of death who know how the soul shrinks from meeting the unknown future.

Experience is a grand teacher and we were then in her school learning that while hope offers the faintest token of refuge, we pause upon the fearful brink of eternity, and look back for rescue.

Mrs. Larimer had climbed into her saddle, her boy placed behind her on the same horse, and started on, accompanied by a party of Indians. I also climbed into my saddle, but was no sooner there than the horse fell to the ground, and I under him, thus increasing the bruises I had already received, and causing me great pain. This accident detained me some time in the rear. A dread of being separated from the only white woman in that awful wilderness filled me with horror.

Soon they had another horse saddled for me, and assisted me to mount him. I looked around for my little Mary. There she stood, a poor helpless lamb, in the midst of blood-thirsty savages. I stretched out my arms for her imploringly. For a moment they hesitated; then, to my unspeakable joy, they yielded, and gave me my child. They then started on, leading my horse; they also gave me a rope that was fastened around the horse's underjaw.

The air was cool and the sky was bright with the glitter of starlight. The water, as it fell over the rocks in the distance, came to our eager ears with a faint, pleasant murmur. All nature seemed peaceful and pitiless in its calm repose, unconscious of our desolate misery; the cry of nightbirds and chirp of insects came with painful distinctness as we turned to leave the valley of the Little Box Elder.

Straining my eyes, I sought to penetrate the shadows of the woods where our fugitive friends might be hiding. The smoldering ruins of our property fell into ashes and the smoke faded away; night had covered the traces of confusion and struggle with her shrouding mantle, and all seemed quiet and unbroken peace.

I turned for a last look, and even the smoke had disappeared; the solemn trees, the rippling water, the soft night wind and the starlight, told no tale of the desolation and death that had gone before; and I rode on in my helpless condition with my child clinging to me, without guide or support, save my trust in God.

V

Plan for Little Mary's Escape

THE Indians left the scene of their cruel rapacity and traveled northward chanting their monotonous war song. After a ride of two miles through tall weeds and bushes, we left the bottom lands and ascended some bluffs. Soon we came to a creek, which was easily forded, and where the Indians quenched their thirst.

The hills beyond began to be more difficult to ascend, and the gorges seemed fearfully deep, as we looked into the black shadows unrelieved by the feeble light of the stars.

In the darkness of our ride I conceived a plan for the escape of little Mary.

I whispered in her childish ear, "Mary, we are only a few miles from our camp, and the stream we have crossed you can easily wade through. I have dropped letters on the way, you know, to guide our friends in the direction we have taken; they will guide you back again, and it may be your only chance of escape from destruction. Drop gently down and lie on the ground for a little while to avoid being seen; then retrace your steps, and may God in mercy go with you. If I can, I will follow you later."

The child, whose judgment was remarkable for her age, readily acceded to my plan; her eyes brightened and her young heart throbbed as she thought of its success.

Watching for an opportunity, I dropped her gently, carefully, and unobserved to the ground, and she lay there while the Indians pursued their way, unconscious of their loss.

To portray my own feelings upon this separation would be impossible. The agony I suffered was indescribable. I was firmly convinced that my course was wise—that I had given her the only chance of escape within my power; yet the terrible uncertainty of what her fate might be in the way before her was almost unbearable.

I continued to think of it so deeply that at last I grew desperate, and resolved to follow her at every risk. Accordingly, watching for an opportunity, I, too, slipped to the ground under the friendly cover of night, and the horse went on without its rider.

My plan was not successful. My flight was soon discovered and the Indians wheeled around and rode back in my pursuit. Crouching in the undergrowth I might have escaped in the darkness were it not for their cunning. Forming a line of forty or fifty abreast, they actually covered the entire ground as they rode toward me.

The horses actually betrayed me when they were frightened at my crouching form. They stopped and reared, thus revealing my hiding place.

With great presence of mind I arose the moment I found myself discovered, and relating my story, the invention of an instant, I succeeded partially in allaying their anger.

I told them that my child had fallen asleep and dropped from the horse; that I had endeavored to call their attention to it, but in vain; and, fearing I would be unable to find her if we rode further, I had jumped down and attempted the search alone.

The Indians used great violence toward me, assuring me that if any further attempts were made to escape, my punishment would be accordingly.

They then promised to send a party out in search of the child when it became light.

Poor little Mary! alone in the wilderness, a little, helpless child; who can portray her terror!

With faith to trust, and courage to dare, that little, trembling form through the long hours of the night kept watch.

The lonely cry of the night bird had no fear in its melancholy scream for the little wanderer who crouched amid the prairie grass. The baying of the gray wolf, as he passed the lonely watcher, might startle, but could not drive the faith from her heart.

Surely God is just and angels will guide the faltering feet to friends and home. How could she but trust that the unseen hands of spirits would guide her from the surrounding perils!

VI

Anxiety, Weariness, and Thirst

T

O TAKE up the thread of my own narrative again and the continuation of my journey with the savages, after the never-to-be-forgotten night when I parted with little Mary and attempted to escape myself, will be to describe to my reader the precipitous and dangerous paths among the great bluffs which we had been approaching, and the dizzy, fearful heights leading over the dark abyss, or the gloomy, terrible gorge, where only an Indian dares to venture.

The blackness of night and the dread of our savage companions added terror to this perilous ride. As we passed the little creek before we plunged into these rocky fastnesses, we had left some scattered woods along its banks.

I remember looking longingly at the dim shelter of these friendly trees, and being possessed by an almost uncontrollable desire to leap from the horse and dare my fate in endeavoring to reach their protecting shade; but the Indians' rifles behind me and my dread of instant death restrained me. And now my attention was attracted by the wild and terrible scenery around us, through which our fearful captors rode at ease, although it seemed impossible for

man or beast to retain a footing over such craggy
peaks and through such rugged ravines.

The cool air and the sound of rippling water
warned us of our nearness to a river; and soon the
savages turned their horses down a steep declivity
that, like a mighty wall, closed in the great bed of
the North Platte.

I saw that the river was rapid and deep, but we
crossed the sands, and without pausing plunged in,
and braved the current.

From the child to my husband was an easy transition; indeed, when I thought of one, the other was
present in my mind; and to mark the path of our
retreat with the letters and papers I dropped on our
way, seemed the only hope I had of his being able
to come to my rescue.

As the horses plunged into the swelling river, I
secretly dropped yet another letter that, I prayed,
might be a clue to the labyrinth through which we
were being led; for I could see by all the Indians'
precautions, that to mislead any who should have
the temerity to attempt our recovery, was the design
of their movements.

They had taken paths inaccessible to white men,
and made their crossing at a point where it would
be impossible for trains to pass, so that they might
avoid meeting emigrants. Having reached the opposite bank they separated into squads, and started in
every direction, except southward, so as to mislead
or confuse pursuers by the various trails.

The band that surrounded and directed us kept to the northward a little by west. I tried to keep the points of compass clearly in mind, because it seemed part of the hope that sustained me.

Mr. Kelly had said that our position on the Little Box Elder was about twelve miles from Deer Creek Station, which lay to the northwest of us. Marking our present course, I tried, by calculating the distance, to keep that position in my mind, for toward it my yearning desire for help and relief turned.

After crossing the river and issuing from the bluffs, we came to a bright, cool stream of water in a lovely valley, which ran through its bosom spreading a delicious freshness all around.

Brilliant flowers opened their gorgeous cups to the coming sunshine, and delicate blossoms hid themselves among the rich shrubbery and at the mossy roots of grand old trees.

The awakening birds soared upward with loud and joyful melodies, and nature rejoiced at the approaching day.

The beauty and loveliness of the scene mocked my sleepless eyes, and despair tugged at my heartstrings; still I made superhuman efforts to appear cheerful for my only refuge was in being submissive and practicing conciliation. My fear of them was too powerful to allow me to give way to emotion for one moment.

There were sentinels stationed at different places to give the alarm in case of anyone approaching to rescue, and I afterward learned that in such a case I would have been instantly murdered.

Next morning I learned, by signs, that Indians had gone out to search for little Mary, scattering themselves over the hills in squads. Those remaining were constantly overlooking their plunder and unrolling bundles taken from our wagons. They indulged their admiration for their spoils in loud and boisterous conversation.

The Indians seemed to select, with a clear knowledge of natural beauty, such localities as seemed best fitted to suggest refreshment and repose.

The scenery through which we had passed was wildly grand; it had now become serenely beautiful, and to a lover of nature, with a mind free from fear and anxiety, the entire picture would have been a dream of delight.

The night of my capture I was ordered to lie down on the ground near a wounded Indian. A circle of them guarded me, and three fierce warriors sat near me with drawn tomahawks.

Reader, imagine my feelings after the terrible scenes of the day previous; the desolate white woman in the power of revengeful savages not daring to speak lest their pent fury should fall on my defenseless head.

My great anxiety now was to preserve my sanity, which threatened to be overcome if I did not arouse myself to hope, and put aside the feeling of despair which at times stole over me. My heart was continually lifted to "Our Father," and, confidently, I now began to feel that prayer would be answered, and that God would deliver me in due season. This nerved me to endure and appear submissive.

At early dawn, I was aroused from my apparent slumbers by the war chief, who sent me out to catch the horses—our American horses being afraid of the savages—and as the animals were those belonging to our train, it was supposed that I could do so readily.

Upon returning, my eyes were gladdened by the sight of my fellow prisoner, who was seated with her boy upon the ground, eating buffalo meat and crackers. I went immediately to her, and while we conversed in low tones, I told her of my intention to escape at the first opportunity. She seemed much depressed, but I endeavored to reassure her, and bidding her hope for the best, went back to where the Indians were making ropes and packing their goods and plunder more securely, preparatory to the succeeding march, which was commenced at an early hour of the day.

We proceeded on our journey until near noon when we halted in a valley not far to the north of Deer Creek Station, and I met this lady again. It was a clear and beautiful valley where we rested until the scorching rays of the sun had faded beneath the blurred horizon.

Being burdened with the gun and bow and arrow of the chief, my tired arms were relieved, and I plead for the privilege of camping here all night for many reasons. One was that we might be overtaken by friends sent to rescue us, and the distance of return would be less if I should be successful in my next attempt to escape.

My entreaties were unavailing; the savages were determined to go forward, and we were quickly mounted and started on. We traveled until sunset, then camped for the night in a secluded valley; we seemed to enter this valley along the base of a wall, composed of bluffs or peaks. Within these circling hills it lay, a green, cool resting place, watered by a bright, sparkling stream.

The moon went down early, and in the dim, uncertain starlight, the heavy bluffs seemed to shut us in on all sides, rising grimly, like guardians, over our imprisoned lines. Blankets were spread, and on these the Indians rested.

I was then led out some distance in the camp, and securely fastened for the night. But before this I remarked to my fellow prisoner my determination to escape that night, if my life were the forfeit, as in every wind I fancied I could hear the voice of little Mary calling me. She entreated me not to leave her, but promising help to her should I be fortunate enough to get free, I sadly bade her good night and went to my allotted place.

In the morning when permitted to rise, I learned that she had disappeared. A terrible sense of isolation closed around me. No one can realize the sensation without in some measure experiencing it.

I was desolate before, but now that I knew myself separated from my only white companion, the feeling increased tenfold and weighed me down with its awful, gloomy horror.

In the heart of the wilderness surrounded by creatures with whom no chord of sympathy was entertained—far from home, friends and the interests of civilized life—the attractions of society, and, above all, separated from husband and loved ones—there seemed but one glimpse of light in all the blackness of despair left, and that was flight.

I listened for every sound while moments appeared hours, and it seemed to me that death in its most terrible form would not be so hard to bear as the torturing agony I then endured.

I murmured broken prayers. I seemed to hear the voices of my husband and child calling out to me. Then I would spring forward with the wild belief that it was real, but later would sink back again overwhelmed with fresh agony.

Arrangements were then made for resuming our journey, and quite soon we were once more on the march. Now, another burden had been added to my almost worn-out frame, the leading of an unruly horse; and my arms were so full of the implements I was forced to carry that I threw away the pipe of the old chief—a tube nearly three feet long, and given me to take care of—which was very unfortunate for me, exciting the wrath and anger of the chief to a terrible degree.

Now they seemed to regard me with a suspicious aversion, and were not so kind as before.

The country we passed over was high, dry, and barren. I rode one horse and led another; and when evening came we had stopped to rest in a grove of great timber where there was a dry creek bed.

Water was obtained by digging in the sand, but the supply was meager and I was allowed none.

The sun began to sink, and the chief was so enraged against me that he told me by signs that I should behold it rise no more.

Grinding his teeth with wrathful anger he made me understand that I was not to be trusted; had once tried to escape; had made them suffer the loss of my child, and that my life would be the forfeit.

A large fire had been built and they all danced around it. Night had begun to darken heavily over me and I stood trembling and horror-struck not knowing that the flame, which the savages capered about, was destined to consume my tortured form.

The pipe of the chief was nowhere to be found, and it was demanded of me to produce it. He used the Indian words, "Chopa-chanopa," uttered in a voice of thunder and with gestures whose meaning was too threatening to be mistaken.

I looked in fear and dismay around me, utterly at a loss to know what was expected, yet dreading the consequences of failing to obey.

Wechela, the Indian boy, who had been so kind, now came to me making the motion of puffing with his lips to aid me. Then I remembered that I had broken the pipe the day before and thrown it away, ignorant of their veneration for the pipe and of its value as a peace offering.

The chief declared that I should die for having caused the loss of his pipe.

An untamed horse was brought and they told me I would be placed on it as a target for their deadliest arrows, and the animal might then run at will, carrying my body where it would.

Helpless and almost dying with terror at my situation, I sank on a rocky seat in their midst. They were all armed and anxiously awaited the signal. They had pistols, bows, and spears; and I noticed that some were ready to raise blazing firebrands to frighten the pawing beast that was to bear me to death.

In speechless agony I pledged my soul to God! Soon I would stand before His throne, and with all the pleading passion of my sinking soul I prayed for both pardon and favor in His precious blood. To Him who had suffered for my sins and risen on high for my justification.

In an instant a lifetime of thought condensed itself into my mind. I could see my old home and hear my mother's voice; and the contrast between the love I had been so ruthlessly torn from, and the hundreds of savage faces, gleaming with ferocity and excitement around me, seemed like the lights and shadows of some weird picture.

Now, I was to die, and I desired, with all the strength of my soul, to grasp the promises of God's mercy and free my parting spirit from all revengeful, earthly thoughts.

In what I almost felt to be my final breath, I prayed for my own salvation and the forgiveness of my enemies; and remembering a purse of money which was in my pocket, knowing that it would decay with my body in the wilderness, I drew it out and, with suffused eyes, divided it among them, though my hands were growing powerless and my sight failing. One hundred and twenty dollars in notes I gave them, telling them its value as I did so, when, to my astonishment, a change came over their faces. They laid their weapons upon the ground, seemingly pleased, and very anxious to understand; then asking me to explain the worth of each note clearly by holding up my fingers.

Eagerly I tried to obey, perceiving the hope their milder manner held out; but my cold hands fell powerless by my side, my tongue refused to utter a sound, and, unconsciously, I sank to the ground utterly insensible to objects around me.

When insensibility gave way to the return of feeling, I was still on the ground where I had fallen, but preparations for the deadly scene were gone, and the savages slumbered on the ground near me by the faint firelight. Crawling into a sitting posture I surveyed the camp and saw hundreds of sleeping forms lying in groups around with sentries set in their places, and no opportunity to escape, even if strength permitted.

Weak and trembling, I sank down, and lay silent till daybreak, when the camp was again put in motion, and, at their bidding, I mounted one horse and led another, as I had done on the day previous.

This was no easy task, for the pack horse, which had not been broken, would frequently pull back so violently as to bring me to the ground. This caused the chief to become fearfully angry, and he would threaten to kill me at once.

Practicing great caution and using strong effort, I would strive to remain in the saddle to avoid the cuffs and blows received.

Whenever the bridle would slip inadvertently from my hand, the chief's blasphemous language would all be English; a sad commentary on the benefits white men confer upon their savage brethren when brought into close contact.

Drunkenness, profanity, and dissolute habits are the lessons of civilization to the red men, and when the weapons we furnish are turned against ourselves, their edge is keen indeed.

Feeling that I had forfeited the goodwill of the Indians, and knowing that the tenure of my life was most uncertain, I dared not to complain, although hunger and devouring thirst tortured me.

The way still led through dry and sandy hills, upon which the sun glared down with exhausting heat, and seemed to scorch life and moisture out of what the rays fell upon. As far as my eyes could see, nothing but burning sand and withering sagebrush or thorny cactus was to be seen. All my surroundings only served to aggravate the thirst which the terrible heat of that long day's ride brought forth to a frenzy.

When in famishing despair I closed my eyes, a cup of cool, delicious drink would seem to be presented to my lips, only to be cruelly withdrawn; and this torture seemed to me like the agony of the rich man, who besought Lazarus for one drop of water to cool his parched tongue.

I thought of all I had been separated from, as it seemed to me, forever, and the torment of the hour reduced me to despair. I wished to die, feeling that the pangs of dissolution could not surpass the anguish of my living death. My voice was almost gone, and only with difficulty could I maintain my seat in the saddle.

Turning my eyes despairingly to my captors I uttered the word "minne," signifying water in their language, and kept repeating it imploringly at intervals. They seemed to hurry forward, and, just at sunset, we came in sight of a grassy valley through which flowed a river, the sight of which came like hope to my almost dying eyes.

A little brook from the hills above found its way into the waters of this greater stream. Soon they dismounted, and, lifting me from my horse, laid me in its shallow bed. I had become almost unconscious, and the cool, delightful element revived me. At first I was not able to drink, but gradually my strength renewed itself, and I found relief from the indescribable pangs of thirst.

The stream by which the Indians camped that night was Powder River; and here, in 1866, Fort Conner was built, which in the following year was named Fort Reno.[1]

[1] Fanny's dates are slightly off. Fort Conner was established in August, 1865, 180 miles northwest of Fort Laramie, but its name was changed to Fort Reno in November of the same year.

VII

My Life Is Spared

THE NAME given to Powder River by the Indians, is "Chahalee Wacapolah." It crosses the country east of the Big Horn Mountains, and from its banks can be seen the snow-capped Cloud Peak rising grandly from its surrounding hills. Between these ranges, that culminate in the queenly, shining crowned height that takes its name from the clouds it seems to pierce, are fertile valleys in which game abounds, and delicious wild fruits in great variety, some of which cannot be surpassed by cultivated orchard products in the richness and flavor they possess, although they ripen in the neighborhood of everlasting snow.

In these valleys the country seems to roll in gentle slopes, presenting to the eye many elements of loveliness and future value.

Powder River, which is a muddy stream, comes from the southern side of the Big Horn Mountains, and takes a southwestern course, and therefore is not a part of the bright channel that combines to feed the Missouri River from the Big Horn range.

This range of the Rocky Mountains possesses two distinctly marked features. First, there is a central or backbone range, which culminates in perpetual snow, where Cloud Peak grandly rises as the chief of all its proud summits. Falling off gradually toward the southern valley, there are similar ranges of the Wind River Mountains beyond.

Between these ranges, and varying in breadth from twelve to twenty-five miles, are fine hunting grounds, abounding in noble orchards of wild fruit of various kinds, and grapes, as well as game of the choicest kind for the huntsman. Notwithstanding its vicinity to snow, there are gentle slopes which present features of peculiar loveliness.

Several miles northwest, and following the sweep of the higher northern range, and six to eight miles outside its general base, a new country opens. Sagebrush and cactus, which for nearly two hundred miles have so largely monopolized the soil, rapidly disappear.

The change, though sudden, is quite beautiful. The transition, which is about a day's ride from the Powder River takes one across a narrow divide. Soon the limpid, transparent, and noisy waters of Deer Fork are reached, and the horses work hard to breast the swift current. The river is so clear that every pebble and fish is seen distinctly on the bottom, and the water so cool that ice in midsummer is no object of desire.

The panorama of natural beauty, and the charms that have endeared this country to the savage will in the future lure the emigrant seeking a home in this new and undeveloped land.

This clear creek is a genuine outflow from the Big Horn Mountains, and is a type of many others, no less pure and valuable, derived from melting snow and from innumerable springs in the mountains.

Rock Creek comes next, with far less pretensions, but is similar in character.

A day's ride to the northward brings the traveler to Crazy Woman's Fork.

This ever-chattering stream receives its yellow hue from the Powder River waters, of which it is a branch.

The country is scarred by countless trails of buffalo, so that what is often called the Indian trail is merely the hoofprint of these animals.

After leaving Powder River, we passed through pine forests, and through valleys rich with beautiful grasses with occasional limpid springs; a seemingly eternal verdure.

I continued to drop papers by the way, hoping they might lead to my discovery, which would have proved fatal had anyone attempted a rescue, as the Indians prefer to kill their captives rather than be forced to give them up.

It was the fifth night of my sojourn with the Indians that I found myself under the weeping willows of Clear Creek.[1]

---

[1]Rock Creek, Crazy Woman's Fork and Clear Creek are all tributaries of the Powder River. The group probably reached Clear Creek somewhere southeast of modern Sheridan and northeast of the town of Buffalo.

The men, weary with travel, and glad to find so good a camping ground, lay down to sleep, leaving a sufficient guard over their captive and at the several outposts.

Our journey hither had been a perilous one to me, unused as I was to the rocky paths between narrow gorges and over masses of broken stone, which the Indian ponies climbed with readiness and ease.

I was led to remark the difference between these ponies and American horses, who could only struggle to find their foothold over such craggy ground, while the ponies led the way, picking their steps up almost perpendicular walls with heavy burdens on their backs.

Travel following the rest at Clear Creek partook of the difficult nature of the mountain passes, and was wearisome in the extreme. The duties forced upon me made life almost too burdensome to be borne, and I found myself looking forward to a respite at the campground.

On the sixth night as I lay on a rock under the shade of some bushes, I meditated on the possibility of escape.

The way was far beyond my reckoning, and the woods where we now were might be infested with wild beasts; but the prospect of my getting away, and being free from the savages, closed my eyes to the terrors of starvation and ravenous animals.

Softly I rose and attempted to steal toward some growing timber; but the watchful chief did not risk his prey so carelessly. His keen eye was on me, and his iron hand grasped my wrist and drew me back. Throwing me fiercely to the ground, he hissed a threat through his clenched teeth, which I momentarily expected him to put into execution, as I lay trembling at his feet.

I felt from this time that my captivity was for life, and a dull despair took possession of me.

Sleep, that balm for happier souls, brought only horrid dreams in which a dreadful future pictured itself; and then the voices of my husband and child seemed calling me to their side, alas! in vain, for when I awoke it was to find myself in the grass of the savage camping ground, watched over by the relentless guard, and shut out from hope of home or civilized life.

My feet were covered with a pair of good shoes, and the chief's brother-in-law gave me a pair of stockings from his stores, which I gladly accepted, never for a moment suspecting that, in doing thus, I was outraging a time-honored custom of the people whom I was with.

The chief saw the gift and made no remark at the time, but immediately after he shot one of his brother-in-law's horses, a bitter quarrel began to unfold.

Realizing that I was the cause of the disagreement, I tremblingly watched the contest, unable to conciliate either combatant, and dreading the wrath of both.

The chief would tolerate no interference, nor would he offer any reparation for the wrong he had inflicted.

His brother-in-law, who became enraged at his arrogance, drew his bow and aimed his arrow at my heart, determined to have satisfaction for the loss of his horse.

I could only cry to God for mercy, and prepare to meet the death which had long hung over my head, when a young Blackfeet, whose name was Jumping Bear, saved me from the approaching doom by adroitly snatching the bow from the savage and hurling it to the earth.

He was named Jumping Bear from the almost miraculous dexterity of some of his feats.

This circumstance plus the Indian mentioned were, in my judgment, instruments in the hand of Providence, quite similar to the saving of Fort Sully[2] from the vengeance and slaughter of the Blackfeet, who had succeeded in gaining the confidence of some of the officers on the Missouri River.

His activity in the attack on our train, and the energy he displayed in killing and pillaging on that occasion, notwithstanding his efforts to make me believe the contrary, forbade me to think there was any sympathy in his interference in my behalf.

[2]Fort Sully was established in September, 1863 as a result of the Sioux uprisings and was initially located on the east bank of the Missouri River approximately three miles below Pierre, South Dakota.

The Indian submitted to his intervention so far that he did not draw his bow again, and my suspense was relieved, for the time, by the gift of a horse from the chief to his brother-in-law, which calmed the fury of the wronged Indian.

It happened that the animal thus given as a peace offering was the pack horse that pulled so uncomfortably against the leading rein, and thus, in the end, I gained by the ordeal through which I had passed, in being relieved of a difficult task.

From the first, I was deprived of every ameliorating comfort that might have rendered my existence bearable.

No tent was spread for me, no rug or coverlet offered me to lie on. The hard earth, sparsely spread with grass, furnished me a couch, and apprehension and regret deprived me of the rest my toilsome life demanded. They offered me no food, and at first I did not dare to ask for it.

This was partially owing to the absence of any natural appetite, an intense weakness and craving constantly for drink being the only signs of the prolonged fast that annoyed me.

The utter hopelessness of my isolation wore on me, driving me almost to madness, and visions of husband and child haunted my brain; sometimes they were full of hope and tauntingly happy; at others, I saw them dying or dead, but always beyond my reach and separated by the impassable barrier of my probably lifelong captivity.

In my weakened condition, the horrors of the burning stake, to which I felt myself being borne nearer as they progressed homeward, appeared like a horrid phantom.

I had been threatened by it since my first effort to flee, and I was led to believe such a punishment was the inevitable consequence of my attempt.

The terrible heat of the days continued, and the road they took was singularly barren of water. The Indians, after drinking plentifully before starting, carry little sticks in their mouths, which they chew constantly, thus creating saliva, and preventing the parching sensation I endured from the want of this knowledge.

The seventh night we entered a singular cañon, apparently well-known to them, as they found horses there, which evidently had been left behind on a former visit.

The Indians had killed an antelope that day, and a piece of raw flesh was allotted me for a meal. We had then traveled in a circuitous route for miles to reach the mouth of this cañon, and entered it just after sundown.

Its gloomy shade was a great relief after the heat of the sun, and it filled my sensitive mind with awe. The sun never seemed to penetrate its depths, and the damp air rose around me like the breath from a dungeon.

Downward we went, as if descending into the bowels of the earth, and the sloping floor we trod was covered with red sand for perhaps the space of half a mile.

We soon struck a rocky pavement, the perpendicular walls of which were of earth; but as we made another turning and entered a large space, the walls seemed to change to stone with projecting arches and overhanging cornices.

The high walls rose above the base so as to nearly meet overhead, and, with their innumerable juttings and irregularities, had the appearance of carved columns supporting a mighty ruin.

Occasionally a faint ray of the fading light struggled with the gloom, into which we plunged deeper and deeper, and often the horses' cautious feet would expose the bones of antelope or deer, drawn thither by the lurking wolf to feed their young.

I was startled with dread at the sight, fearing that they might be human bones with which mine would soon be mingled.

The increasing darkness had made it necessary for the Indians to carry torches, which they did, lighting up the grotesque grandeur of earth and rock through which they passed by the weird glare of their waving brands.

Upon arriving at the place they selected to be our campground, they prepared fires, whose fantastic gleams danced upon the rocky walls, and added a magical splendor to their wondrous tracery. The ghostly grandeur of these unfrequented shades cannot be described, however the effect was marvelous.

They seem to shadow forth the outline of carving and sculpture, and in the uncertain firelight have all the effect of some old-time temple, whose art and glory will live forever, even when its classic stones are dust.

Here I found water for my parched lips, which was more grateful to my weary senses than any natural phenomenon; and sinking on a moss-grown rock near the trickling rill that sank away in the sand beyond, I found slumber in that strange, fantastic solitude.

I was aroused by a whistling sound, and, gathering myself up, looked fearfully around me. Two flaming eyes seemed to pierce the darkness like a sword. I shuddered and held my breath, as a long, lithe serpent wound past me, trailing its shining length through the damp sand and moving slowly out of sight among the dripping vines.

After that I slept no more; and when I saw the struggling light of day pierce the rocky opening above, I gladly hailed the safety of the sunshine, even though it brought sorrow, distress, and toil.

When we rose in the morning, we left the cañon by the path we entered, as it seemed to have no other outlet, and then journeyed on.

VIII

Arrival at the Indian Village

ON THE twentieth of July we had nearly reached the Indian village, when we stopped for the night. As usual, when such a locality could be gained, we camped near a stream of good water.

Here was a current of sparkling, rippling water, fresh from the melting snow of the mountain. It was a warm, still night. Soon the sky began to darken strangely, and great ragged masses of clouds hung low over the surrounding hills. The air grew heavy, relieved occasionally by a deep gust of wind that died away and was succeeded by an ominous calm. Then a low, muttering thunder jarred painfully on the ear. My shattered nerves recoiled at the prospect of the coming storm. From a child I had been timid of lightning, and now its forked gleam filled me with dismay in my unsheltered helplessness.

The Indians, seeing the approaching tempest, prepared for it by collecting and fastening their horses and covering their firearms and ammunition, and lying flat on the earth themselves. I crouched, too, but could not escape the terrible glare of the lightning, and the roar of the awful thunder grew deafening.

On came the storm with startling velocity, and

the dreaded artillery of heaven boomed overhead, followed closely by blinding flashes of light; and the velocity of the whirlwind seemed to arise in its might so as to add desolation to the terrible scene.

When the vivid gleams lit up the air, enormous trees could be seen bending under the fierceness of the blast, and great white sheets of water burst out of the clouds, as if intent on deluging the world. Every element in nature united in terrific warfare, and the security of the earth seemed denied to me while I clung to its flooded bosom, and, blinded by lightning and shocked by the incessant roaring of the thunder and the wild ravaging of the ungovernable wind, felt myself but a tossed atom in the great confusion, and could only cling to God's remembering pity in silent prayer.

Huge trees were bent to the earth and broken; others, snapped off like twigs, were carried through the frenzied air. Some forest monarchs were left completely bare of leaves or boughs, like desolate old age stripped of its honors.

The rain had already swelled the little creek into a mighty stream, that rolled its dark, angry waters with fury and added its sullen roar to the howlings of the storm. I screamed, but my voice was lost even to myself in the mightier ones of the furious elements. For three long hours—three long, never-to-be-forgotten hours—the storm raged in its fury, and in those hours I felt I had lived a lifetime! Then, to my joy, it began to abate, and soon I beheld the twinkling stars through rents in the driving clouds, while the flashing lightning and the roaring thunder, gradually becoming less and less frightening to the eye and ear, told me the devastating storm was speeding on toward the east. Later, when, at dawn of day, the waters were assuaged, the thunder died away and the lightning was chained in its cell, the scene was that of indescribable desolation. The wind had gone home; daylight had changed it from a raging giant into but a meek prisoner, and led it moaning to a cavern in the eastern hills. A strangely solemn calm seemed to take the place of the wild conflict; but the track of destruction was there, and the swollen water and felled trees, the scattered boughs and uprooted saplings, told the story of the havoc of the storm.

It was a night of horror we all suffered through, and I offered a prayer of thanks as I greeted the returning day, that once more gave me the comfort of light, now almost my only solace. My position had grown more bitter as the chief's savage-like exultation in my capture and safe abduction increased as we neared the camp where their families were, and where I feared my fate would be decided by bloodshed or the fearful stake.

On the twenty-first of July we left camp early, the day being cool and favorable for traveling. Our route lay over rolling prairie, interspersed with extensive tracts of marsh, which, however, we easily avoided crossing. A few miles brought us to a high, broken ridge, stretching nearly in a north and south direction. After reaching the top of the ridge, we sighted a large herd of buffalo, quietly feeding upon the bunch, or buffalo grass, which they prefer to all other kinds. These animals are short-sighted, and scent the approach of an enemy before they can see him, and thus, in their curiosity, often start to meet him, until they approach near enough to ascertain to their satisfaction whether there be danger in a closer acquaintance. In this case they decided in the affirmative, and, when they had once fairly made us out, lost no time in increasing the distance between us, starting on a slow, clumsy trot, which was soon quickened to a gait that generally left most pursuers far in the rear.

But the Indians and their horses are trained buffalo hunters, and soon succeeded in surrounding a number. They ride alongside their victim, and, leveling their guns or arrows, send their aimed shot in the region of the heart, then ride off to a safe distance, avoiding the desperate lunge which a wounded buffalo seldom fails to make. Then, the shaggy beast, shaking his head crowned with horns of most formidable strength, stands at bay with eyes darting, savage and defiant, as he looks at his human foe. The hunters do not shoot again, but wait patiently until their victim grows weak from loss of blood, and, staggering, falls upon his knees, makes a final effort to stand erect, but then, collapsing once more, rolls over on his side, dead.

Sometimes these animals number tens of thousands in droves. The Indians often, for the mere sport, make an onslaught, killing great numbers of them, and then have a plentiful feast of "ta-tonka," as they call buffalo meat. They use no economy in food. It is always a feast or a famine; and they seem equally able to gorge or fast. Each man selects the part of the animal he has killed that best suits his own taste, and leaves the rest to decay or be eaten by wolves, thus wasting their own game, and often suffering privation in consequence.

They gave me a knife and motioned me to help myself to the feast. I did not accept, thinking then it would never be possible for me to attempt to eat uncooked meat.

They camped here overnight; then started early the next morning. We were now nearing the village where the Indians belonged.

Jumping Bear, the young Indian who had shown me so many marks of goodwill, again made his appearance with a sad expression on his face, and that day would ride in silence by my side; which was an act of great condescension on his part, for these men rarely thus equalize themselves with women, but ride in advance.

We had traveled nearly three hundred miles, and, despite my fears, I began to rejoice in the prospect of arriving among women, even though they were savages; and a dawning hope that I might find pity and companionship with others of my own sex, however separated their lives and customs might be.

I had read of the dusky maidens of romance. I thought of all the characters of romance and history, wherein the nature of the red man is enshrined in poetic beauty. The untutored nobility of soul, the brave generosity, the simple dignity untrammeled by the hollow conventionalities of civilized life, all rose mockingly before me, and the heroes of my youthful imagination passed through my mind in strange contrast with the flesh and blood realities into whose hands I had fallen.

The stately Logan, the fearless Philip, the bold Black Hawk, the gentle Pocahontas: how unlike the greedy, cunning, and cruel savages who had so ruthlessly torn me from my friends![1]

Truly, those pictures of the children of the forest that adorn the pages of the novelist are delightful conceptions of the airy fancy, fitted to charm the mind. They amuse and beguile the hours they invest with their interest; but the true red man, as I saw him, does not exist between the pages of many volumes. He roams his native wastes, and to once

[1]Logan was a chief of the Mingo in the Ohio country, a leading participant in Lord Dunmore's War of 1774 and noted for his movingly eloquent plea on behalf of his people. Chief of the Wampanoag tribe, Philip formed a confederacy against the New England colonies in King Philip's War, 1675–76, of which he was a victim. Black Hawk was the great Sauk leader who waged a tragic campaign against the whites in Illinois in 1832. Pocahontas was the Powhatan woman who in legend saved John Smith from death and subsequently married the Englishman John Rolfe.

encounter and study him there, so much must be sacrificed that I was unable to appreciate the knowledge I was gaining at such a price.

Notwithstanding all I had seen and experienced, I do recall much that was gentle and faithful in the character associated with the Indian women. Perhaps I might be able to find one whose sympathy and companionship could be wrought upon to the extent of aiding me in some way to escape. I became hopeful with the thought, and almost forgot my terror of the threats of my captors in my desire to see the friendly faces of Indian women.

The country around was rich and varied. Beautiful birds appeared in the trees and flowers of variety and fragrance nodded on their stems. Wild fruits were abundant and I plucked roses and fruit for food, while my savage companions feasted on raw meat. They did not seem to care for fruit, and urged me to eat meat with them. I refused because of its being raw. A young Indian, guessing the cause of my refusal to eat, procured a kettle, made a fire, cooked some, and offered it to me. I tried to eat of it to please them, since they had taken the trouble to prepare a special dish, but owing to the filthy manner in which it was prepared, a very small portion satisfied me.

We were now nearing a river, which, from its locality, must have been the Tongue River, where we found refreshing drink, and rested for a short time. The Indians gave me to understand that when we crossed this stream, and a short distance beyond, we would be at their home.[2]

Here they paused to dress, so as to make a gay appearance and imposing entrance into the village. Except when in full dress, an Indian's wearing apparel consists only of a buffalo robe, which is also part of a fine toilet. It is quite inconveniently disposed about the person, without any fastening, and must be held in position with the hands.

Here the clothing seized from our train was brought into great demand, and each warrior that had been fortunate enough to possess himself of any article of our dress, now arrayed himself to the best advantage the garments and their limited ideas of civilization would permit. In several instances when the toilet was considered complete, changes for less attractive articles of display were made with companions who had not been so fortunate as others in the division of the goods, that they might also share in the sport afforded by this derisive display.

Their peculiar ideas of tasteful dress rendered them grotesque in appearance. One darkened face appeared under the shade of my hat, smiling with obvious satisfaction at the superiority of his decorations over those of his less fortunate companions; another was shaded from the scorching rays of the

[2]Since the village seems to have been somewhere between the Heart and the Cannonball Rivers in North Dakota, the river Fanny calls the Tongue was too far east and may have been the Little Missouri.

sun by a tiny parasol, and the brown hand that held it aloft was thinly covered by a silk glove, which was about the only article of clothing, except the invariable breechcloth, that the warrior wore.

Vests and other garments were put on with the lower part upward; and they all displayed remarkable versatility in the arrangement of their decorations. They seemed to think much of their stolen goods, some of which were frivolous, while others simply worthless.

Decorating themselves by way of derision, each noble warrior endeavored to outdo the other in splendor, which was altogether estimated by color, and not by texture. Their horses were also decked in the most ridiculous manner.

Ottawa, or Silver Horn, the war chief, was arrayed in complete costume. He was quite old, over seventy-five, partially blind, and under the medium height. He was ferocious and savage looking, and now, when in costume, looked frightful. His face was red with stripes of black, and around each eye a circlet of bright yellow. His long, black hair was divided into two braids with a scalp lock on top of the head. His ears held great brass wire rings, six full inches in diameter, and chains and beaded necklaces were suspended from his neck. Armlets and bracelets of brass, together with a string of bears' claws, completed his jewelry. He also wore leggings of deer skin, and a shirt of the same material, beautifully ornamented with beads, and fringed with scalp locks, which he claimed to have been taken from his enemies, both red and white. Across his shoulders hung a great, bright-colored quilt, that had been taken from our stores. He wore a crown of eagle feathers on his head; also a long plume of feathers descending from the back of the crown.

His horse, a noble-looking animal, was no less gorgeously arrayed. His ears were pierced, like his master's, and his neck was encircled by a wreath of bears' claws, taken from animals that the chief had slain. Some bells and a human scalp hung from his mane, forming together, thus arrayed, a museum of the trophies of the old chief's prowess on the war-path, and of skill in the chase.

When all was arranged, the chief mounted his horse and rode on in triumph toward the village, highly elated over the possession of his white captive, whom he never looked back at or deigned to notice, except to chastise on account of her slowness, which was unavoidable, as I rode a jaded horse and could not keep pace.

The entire Indian village poured forth to meet us, amid song and wild dancing in the most enthusiastic manner; flourishing flags and weapons of war in frenzied joy as we entered the village, which, stretched for miles along the banks of the stream. It resembled a vast military encampment, with the wigwams covered with white skins, like Sibley tents in shape and size, ranged without regard to order, but facing one point of the compass.

We penetrated through the irregular settlement for over a mile, accompanied by the enthusiastic escort of men, women, and children.

I rode in the center of a double column of Indians and directly in the rear of the chief until we reached the door of his lodge, when several of his wives came out to meet him. He had six, but the senior one remained in the tent, while a younger one was absent with the Farmer or Grosventre Indians. Their salutation is very much in the manner of the Mexicans; the women crossed their arms on the chief's breast, and smiled.

They met me in silence, but with looks of great astonishment.

I got down as directed, and followed the chief into the great lodge or tent, distinguished from the others by its superior ornaments. It was decorated with brilliantly colored porcupine quills and a terrible fringe of human scalp locks, the results of several battles with the Pawnees.

On one side was depicted a representation of the Good Spirit, rude in design and daubed with colors. On the other side was portrayed the figure of the spirit of evil in like manner. The Indians believe in these two deities and pay their homage to them. The first they consider to be entirely benevolent and kind, but the second is filled with vile tricks and wicked ways.

They fear him and consider it only safe to propitiate him occasionally by obedience to his evil will.

This may account for some of their worst ferocities and explain that horrible brutality of nature which they so often exhibit.

The senior wife, who had remained in the lodge, met her husband with the same salutation as the others had done.

I was shown to a seat on a buffalo skin opposite the entrance. The chief's spoil was brought in for division by his elderly spouse.

As it was spread out before them, the women gathered admiringly around, and proved their peculiarities of taste. The love of finery had a counterpart in these forest belles, as well defined as if they had been city ladies. Eagerly they watched every new article displayed, grunting their approval, until their senior companion seized a piece of cloth, declaring that she meant to retain it for herself.

This occasioned dissatisfaction, which soon ripened to rebellion among them, and they contended for a just distribution of the goods. The elder matron, following her illustrious husband's plan in quelling such outbreaks, caught her knife from her belt, sprang in among them, vowing that she was the oldest and had the right to govern, and threatening to kill everyone if there was the least objection offered to her decrees. I had so hoped to find sympathy and pity among these artless women of the forest, but instead, cowed and trembling, I sat, scarcely daring to breathe.

The chief noticed my fear and shrinking posture,

Sioux Indian Village
Courtesy Siouxland Heritage Museums

and smiled. Then he rose and made a speech, which had its effect. The women became quiet. Presently an invitation arrived for the chief to go to a feast, and he rose to comply.

I followed his departing figure with regret, for, terrible as he and his men had been, the women seemed still more formidable, and I feared to be left alone with them, especially because of the hot temper and ready knife of the elder squaw.

Great crowds of curious Indians came flocking in to stare at me. The women brought their children. Some of them, whose fair complexion astonished me, I afterward learned were the offspring of fort marriages.

One fair little boy who, with his mother, had just returned from Fort Laramie, came close to me. Finding the squaw could speak a few words in English, I addressed her and was told, in reply to my questions, that she had been the wife of a captain there, but because his white wife would soon be arriving from the East, his Indian wife was to return to her people. She did so, taking her child with her. The little boy was outfitted completely in military clothing, even to the stripe on his pantaloons. He appeared to be a very bright, attractive child of about four years.

It was a very sad thought for me to realize that a parent could part with such a child, committing it forever to live in barbarous ignorance, and rove the woods among savages with the impress of his own superior race, so strongly mingled with his Indian origin. I saw many other fair-faced little children, and heard the sad story from their mothers, and was deeply pained to see their pale, pinched features as they cried for food when there was none to be had. On many occasions they are cruelly treated by the full-blooded and larger children because of their unfortunate birth.

As soon as the question of property was decided between the women of the chief's family, they became more kindly disposed toward me, and one of them brought me a dish of meat. Many others followed her example, even those from the neighboring lodges. All really seemed to pity me, and showed great evidences of compassion. They tried to express their sympathy in signs, because I had been torn from my own people and compelled to come on such a long, fatiguing journey. They examined me over and over again, particularly my dress, hands, and feet. Then, to their great surprise, they discovered my bruised and almost broken limbs that occurred when first taken, also from the fall of the horse the first night of my captivity, and proceeded at once to dress my wounds.

I was just beginning to rejoice in the dawning kindness that seemed to soften their swarthy faces when a messenger from the war chief arrived, accompanied by a small party of young warriors sent to conduct me to the chief's presence. I did not at first comprehend the summons, and, as every fresh announcement only awakened new fears, I dreaded to comply, yet dared not refuse. Seeing my hesitation, the senior wife allowed a little daughter of the chief's, whose name was Yellow Bird, to accompany me, and I was then conducted to several feasts, at each of which I was received with kindness, and promised good will and protection. It was here that the chief himself first condescended to talk kindly to me, and this and the companionship of the child, Yellow Bird, who seemed to approach me with a trusting grace and freedom unlike the scared shyness of Indian children generally, inspired hope.

The chief here told me that henceforth I could call Yellow Bird my own, to take the place of my little girl that had been killed. I did not at once comprehend all of his meaning, still it gave me some hope of security.

At nightfall, after we came back to the lodge, which they told me I must henceforth regard as home, I found the elder women busily pounding a post into the ground, and my fears were at once aroused. I was always ready to become afraid when something suggested a token of some evil. On the contrary, it was simply some household arrangement of her own, for presently, putting on a camp kettle, she built a fire and caused water to boil, and drew a tea of which she gave me a portion, assuring me that it would cure the tired and weary feeling and secure me a good rest.

This proved true. Soon a deep drowsiness began

Sioux Indian Woman
Courtesy Newberry Library

81

to steal over the weary captive. My bed of furs was shown me. Yellow Bird was told to share my couch with me, and from this time on she was my constant attendant. I laid down and the wife of the chief tenderly removed my moccasins, and I slept sweetly—the first honest sleep I had enjoyed in many weary nights.

Before my eyes closed in slumber my heart rose in gratitude unspeakable to God for his great and immeasurable mercy.

I readily adapted myself to my new position. The chief's three sisters shared the lodge with us.

The following day commenced my labors, and the chief's wife seemed to feel a protecting interest in me.

The day of the twenty-fifth of July was observed by continual feasting in honor of the safe return of the braves.

There was a large tent made by putting several together, where all the chiefs, medicine men, and great warriors met for consultation and feasting. I was invited to attend, and was given an elevated seat, while the rest of the company all sat cross-legged upon the ground preparatory to the feast being dealt out.

In the center of the circle was erected a flagstaff with many scalps, trophies, and ornaments fastened to it. Near the foot of the flagstaff were placed, in a row on the ground, several large kettles in which was prepared the feast. Also, on the ground near the kettles, was a bevy of wooden bowls in which the meat was to be served. In front there were two or three women, who were acting as waiters to light the pipes for smoking as well as to serve the food. While I remained seated, thousands began climbing and crowding around for a peep at me. At length, the chief arose in a very handsome costume, and addressed the audience. I could understand but little of his meaning, but he often pointed to me.

Several others also made speeches that sounded the same to me. I sat trembling with fear at these strange proceedings, fearing they were deliberating upon a plan of putting me to some cruel death to finish their amusement. It is impossible to describe my feelings on that day, as I sat in the midst of those wild, savage people. Soon a handsome pipe was lit and brought to the chief to smoke. He took it, and after presenting the stem to the north, the south, the east, and the west, and then to the sun that was over his head, uttered a few words, drew a few whiffs, then passed it around through the whole group, who all smoked. This smoking was conducted with the strictest adherence to exact and established form, and the entire feast was conducted in the most positive silence.

The lids were raised from the kettles, which were all filled with dog's meat that had been well cooked and made into some sort of stew. Each guest had a large wooden bowl placed before him with a quantity of dog's flesh enmeshed in a profusion of soup or rich gravy. A large spoon, made of buffalo horn, rested in the dish.

In this most difficult and painful dilemma I sat witnessing the solemnity; my dish was given me, and the absolute necessity of eating it was painful to contemplate. I tasted it a few times after much urging, and then resigned my dish, which was taken and passed around with others to every part of the group, who all ate heartily. In this way the feast ended, and all retired silently and gradually until the ground was left to the waiters.

The women signified to me that I should feel highly honored by being called to feast with chiefs and great warriors; and seeing the spirit in which it was given, I could not but treat it respectfully, and receive it as a very high and marked compliment.

Since I witnessed it on this occasion, I have been honored with numerous entertainments of the kind, and all conducted in the same solemn and impressive manner.

As far as I could see and understand, I feel authorized to pronounce the dog-feast a truly religious ceremony, wherein the superstitious Indian sees fit to sacrifice his faithful companion to bear testimony to the sacredness of his vows of friendship for the Great Spirit. He first offers a portion of meat to his deity, then places it on the ground to remind him of the sacrifice and solemnity of the offering.

The dog, among all Indian tribes, is more esteemed and more valued than among any part of the civilized world. The Indian has more time to devote to his company, and his untutored mind more nearly assimilates to the nature of his faithful servant.

The flesh of these dogs, though apparently relished by the Indians, is undoubtedly inferior to venison and buffalo meat, of which feasts are constantly made, and where friends are invited, as they are in civilized society, to a pleasant and convivial party. Using this fact alone, it would seem clear that they have some extraordinary motive for feasting on the flesh of that useful and faithful animal in the instance I have been describing.

Their village was well supplied with fresh and dried meat of the buffalo and deer. The dog-feast is given, I believe, by all tribes in America, and in them all this faithful animal, as well as the horse, is sacrificed in several different ways to appease offended spirits or deities, whom it is considered necessary that they should conciliate in this way. This is invariably done by giving the best in the herd or the kennel.

That night was spent in dancing. It seemed quite wild and furious to me. I was led into the center of the circle, and assigned the painful duty of holding above my head human scalps fastened to a little pole. The dance was kept up until near morning, when all repaired to their respective lodges. The three kind sisters of the chief were there to convey me to mine.

IX

A Running Battle with the Soldiers

THE next morning the whole village was in motion. The warriors were going to battle against a white enemy, they said, and old men, women, and children were sent out in different directions to a place of safety as designated by the chief. Everything was soon moving. With the rapidity of custom the tent poles were lowered and the tents rolled up. The cooking utensils were put together and laid on crossbeams connecting the lower ends of the poles as they trail the ground from the horses' sides, to which they are attached. Dogs, too, are made useful in this exodus, and started off with smaller burdens dragging after them in the same manner that horses are packed.

The whole village was in commotion; children screaming or laughing; dogs barking or growling under their heavy burdens; squaws running hither and thither, taking down tipi poles and packing up everything; then leading away horses and dogs with huge bundles.

The small children are placed in sacks of buffalo skin and hung upon saddles or their mothers' backs. The wrapped up lodges, which are held tightly by thongs, are fastened to the poles on the horses' backs, together with other articles of domestic use, and upon these are seated women and older children. In order to guide the horse one of the women goes before, holding the bridle and carrying on her back a load nearly as large as the horse carries.

Women and children are sometimes seated on horses while holding in their arms every variety of plunder including little dogs and other forlorn and hungry looking pets. In this rather unsightly manner, sometimes two or three thousand families are transported many miles during the same migration, and, because all are in motion at the same time, the cavalcade extends for a great distance.

The men and boys are not so unsightly in their appearance, being mounted upon good horses and the best Indian ponies. They ride in groups, leaving the women and children to trudge along with the burdened horses and dogs.

The number and utility of these faithful dogs is at times astonishing, as they total in the hundreds, each bearing a portion of the general household goods. Two poles, about ten or twelve feet long, are attached to the shoulders of a dog, leaving one end of each dragging upon the ground. On these poles a small burden is carried, and with it the faithful canine jogs along, looking neither to the right nor to the left, but apparently intent upon reaching the end of his journey. These faithful creatures are under the ever-watchful eyes of the women and children, and their pace is oftentimes encouraged with admonitions as well as vigorous and zealous use of whips applied to their limbs and sides. It was quite painful to me to see these poor animals taken from their natural avocation and forced to a slavish life of labor, and compelled to travel along with their burdens; yet, when this change has been made, they become worthless as hunters or watchers, and even for the purpose of barking, being reduced, instead, to beasts of burden. It was not uncommon to see a great wolfish-looking dog moodily jogging along with a lot of cooking utensils on one side, and on the other a crying papoose for a balance, while his sulking companion toils on, supporting upon his back a quarter of antelope or elk, and is followed by an old woman or some children, who keep at bay all refractory dogs who run loose, occasionally showing their superiority by snapping and snarling at their more unfortunate companions.

This train was immensely large, nearly the whole Sioux nation having concentrated there for the purpose of war. The chief's sisters brought me a saddled horse, then told me to mount and accompany the already moving column that seemed to be spreading far over the hills to the northward. We toiled on all day. Late in the afternoon we arrived at the ground of encampment where we rested while awaiting further orders from the warriors, who had gone to battle and would afterward join us there.

I had no means of informing myself at that time as to with whom the war was raging, but afterward learned that General Sully's army was pursuing the Sioux, and that the engagement was with his men.[1]

In three days the Indians returned to camp and entered on a course of feasting and rejoicing that caused me to believe that they had suffered very little loss in the affray.

They passed their day of rest in this sort of entertainment; and here I first witnessed the scalp dance, a ceremonial which did not increase my respect or confidence in the tender mercies of my captors.

This performance is only gone through at night and by the light of torches. Consequently, its terrible characteristics are heightened by the fantastic gleams of the lighted brands.

The women, too, took part in the dance, and I was forced to mingle in the fearful festivity, painted and dressed especially for the occasion and holding a staff from the top of which hung several scalps.

The braves came vauntingly forth with the most extravagant boasts of their wonderful prowess and courage in war, at the same time brandishing weapons in their hands with the most fearful contortions and threatenings.

[1] The son of the renowned portrait painter Thomas Sully and a graduate of West Point, Alfred Sully served in the Mexican War, in campaigns in Florida and Oregon, and with Harney against the Sioux in 1856. Much decorated while with the Army of the Potomac during the Civil War, he was pulled from his brigade at Chancellorsville because of his Indian-fighting experience. Now he moved against the Sioux at Killdeer Mountain, smashed their villages and pursued them through the North Dakota Bad Lands.

A number of young women came with them, carrying the trophies of their friends, which they held up high as the warriors jumped in a circle, while brandishing their weapons and whooping and yelling the fearful war cry in a most frightful manner. All were jumping upon both feet at the same time with simultaneous stamping and motions with their weapons while keeping exact time. Their gestures looked as if they were actually cutting and carving each other to pieces as they uttered their fearful, sharp yell. They became furious as they grew more excited, their faces becoming distorted to the utmost; their glaring eyes protruded with a fiendish, indescribable appearance while they grind their teeth and attempt to imitate the hissing, gurgling sound of death in battle. Furious and faster grows the stamping until the sight is more like a picture of fiends in a carnival of battle than anything else to which the war dance can be compared.

No description can fully convey the terrible sight in all its fearful barbarity, as the bloody trophies of their victory are brandished aloft in the light of the flickering blaze and their distorted forms were half concealed by darkness. The object for which the scalp is taken is exultation and proof of valor and success. My pen is powerless to portray my feelings during this terrible scene.

This country seemed scarred by countless trails where the Indian ponies have dragged lodge poles during their change of habitations or hunting. The

General Alfred Sully
Courtesy Minnesota Historical Society

antipathy of the Indian to the white man's occupation or invasion of its land is very intense and bitter. The felling of timber, killing of buffalo, traveling of a train, or any other indication of permanent possession by the white man excites deadly hostility. It is their last hope; if they yield and give up this, they will have to die or ever after be governed by the white man's laws; consequently they lose no opportunity to kill, steal from, or harass the whites when they can do so.

The wild game still clings to its favorite haunts, and the Indian must press upon the steps of the white man or lose all hope of independence. Herds of elk proudly stand with antlers held erect as if charmed by music, or as if curious to understand this strange inroad upon their long-secluded parks of pleasure. The mountain sheep look down from belting crags that skirt the perpendicular northern face of the mountains, and yield no rival of their many charms or excellence for food. The black and white-tail deer and antelope are ever present, while the hare and the rabbit, the sage hen, and the prairie chicken are nearly trodden down before they yield to the intrusion of the stranger.

Brants, wild geese, and ducks multiply and people the waters of beautiful lakes, and many of the streams. The grizzly and cinnamon bears are often killed and give up their rich material for the hunter's profit. The buffalo, in numberless herds of tens of thousands, sweep back and forth, filling the valley as far as the eye can reach, and adding their value to the red man for food, habitation, fuel, and clothing. The Big Horn River and streams beyond are plentifully supplied with various kinds of fish. The country seems to be filled with wolves, which pierce the night air with their howls, but, like the beavers whose dams incumber the smaller streams, and the otter are forced to yield their nice coats for the Indian as well as the white man's luxury.

The Indians felt that the proximity of the troops and the inroads made through their best hunting grounds would prove disastrous to them and their future hopes of prosperity. Soon again they were making preparations for battle; and again, on the eighth of August, the warriors set forth on the warpath, and this time the action seemed to draw ominously near our encampment.

An Indian boy died the night before and was buried rather hastily in the morning. The body was wrapped in some window curtains that once draped my windows at Geneva. There was also a red blanket and many beads and trinkets deposited on an elevated platform with the moldering remains, and the bereaved mother and relatives left the lonely spot with loud lamentations. There seemed to be great commotion and great anxiety in the movements of the Indians. Presently I could hear the sound of battle; and the echoes that came back to me from the reports of the guns in the distant hills warned me of the near approach of my own people.

My heart became prey to wildly conflicting emotions as we hurried on in great desperation, which even forbade me to turn my head and look in the direction of the battle. Once I broke the rule and was severely punished for it. They kept their eyes upon me and were particularly cross and unkind.

Panting for rescue, yet fearing for its accomplishment, I passed the day. The smoke of action was now rising up from the hills beyond and the Indians began to realize that danger was imminent and hurried on in great consternation.

General Sully's soldiers appeared in close proximity, and I could see them charging on the Indians, who, according to their habits of warfare, skulked behind trees while sending their bullets and arrows vigorously forward into the enemy's ranks. I was kept in advance of the moving column of women and children, who were hurrying on, crying and famishing for water while trying to keep out of the line of firing.

It was late at night before we stopped our pace. Finally, we reached the lofty banks of a noble river, but it was some time before a break in the rocky shores could be located from which we were able to reach the water and enjoy a delicious draught. It was a luxury that we were glad to share with our panting horses.

We had traveled far and fast all day long without cessation, through dense clouds of smoke and dust, parched by a scorching sun. My face was blistered from the burning rays, as I had been compelled to go with my head uncovered after the fashion of all Indian women. I had not had a drop of water during the entire day.

Reluctant to leave the long-desired acquisition, the Indians all lay down beneath the tall willows close to the stream, and slept the sleep of the weary. The horses lingered near, nipping the tender blades of grass that sparsely bordered the stream.

It was not until next morning that I thought of how they should cross the river, which I figured to have been the Missouri. It was not very wide but confined between steep banks. It seemed to be deep and quite rapid. To my joy the Indians did not risk swimming at that location, but went further down where all plunged in and swam across, leading my horse. I was extremely frightened and pleaded to Heaven for mercy. Later that morning we entered a gorge that contained a mass of huge fragments which had fallen from the mountains above. They led my horse and followed each other closely, and with as much speed as possible, as we were still pursued by the troops. During the day some two or three warriors were brought in wounded. I was called to see them and assist in dressing their wounds. This being my first experience of the kind, I was at some loss to know what was best to do; but, seeing in it a good opportunity to raise myself in their esteem, I tried to impress them with my superior knowledge of surgery, and as nurse or medicine woman. I felt now, from their menacing glances, that my life was not safe, since we were being so closely pursued.

My feelings, all this time, cannot be described, particularly when I could hear the sound of the big guns, as the Indians term cannon. I felt that the soldiers had surely come for me and would overtake us, and my heart leaped with joy at the thought of deliverance, but sunk proportionately when the warriors came to me bearing their many trophies: reeking scalps and bloody army uniforms, which told a sad story to my aching heart. One day I might be cheered by strong hope of approaching relief, then again I would have such assurance of my enemies' success as would sink me correspondingly low in despair. For some reason deception seemed to be the Indians' peculiar delight; whether they did it to gratify an insatiable thirst for revenge in themselves or to keep me more reconciled and more willing and patient to abide, was something I was unable to determine.

The feelings occasioned by my disappointment in their success can be better imagined than described, but imagination, even in its most extravagant flights, can but poorly picture the horrors that met my view during these running occasions.

My constant experience was hope deferred that maketh the heart sick. It was most tantalizing and painful to my spirit to be so near our forces and the flag of liberty, and yet be a prisoner and helpless.

On, and still on, we were forced to fly to a place

known among them as the Bad Lands, a section of country so wildly desolate and barren as to induce the belief that its present appearance is the effect of volcanic action.[2]

Everything has a ruined look, as if vegetation and life had formerly existed there, but had been suddenly interrupted by some violent commotion of nature. A terrible blight, like the fulfilling of an ancient curse, darkens the surface of the gloomy landscape, and the desolate, ruinous scene might well represent the entrance to the infernal shades described by classic writers.

A choking wind blows continually, and sand fills the air as dry and blinding dust.

The water is sluggish and dark, and apparently life-destroying in its action, because all that lies around its moistened limits has assumed the form of petrifaction. Rocks seemed as if they had formerly held both animal and vegetable life, and their change will no doubt become a subject of interesting speculation to enterprising men of science, who penetrate these mournful shades to discover toads, snakes, birds, and a variety of insects, together with plants, trees, and many curiosities, all petrified and having the appearance of stone. I was startled by the strange and wonderful sights.

The terrible scarcity of water and grass urged us forward, and General Sully's army in the rear gave

[2]These are the "Mauvaises Terres" of the Little Missouri River in southwestern North Dakota.

us no rest. The following day or two we were driven so far northward, and became so imminently imperiled by the pursuing forces, that the Indians were obliged to leave all their earthly effects behind them, and swim the Yellowstone River for life. By this time the ponies were completely famished for want of food and water, so jaded that it was with great difficulty and hard blows that we could urge them on at all.

When Indians are pursued closely, they evince a desperate and reckless desire to save themselves without regard to property or provisions.

They throw away everything that will impede flight, and all natural instinct seems lost in fear. We had left, in our compulsory haste, immense quantities of plunder, even lodges standing, which proved immediate help, but in the end a terrible loss.

General Sully with his entire troop stopped to destroy the property, thus giving us an opportunity to escape, which saved us from falling into his hands, as otherwise we inevitably would have done.

The soldiers consumed one day in collecting and burning the Indian lodges, blankets, provisions, etc., and the Indians used that advantageously in getting beyond their reach. Indians travel constantly in time of war, ranging over vast tracts of country, and prosecuting their battles or skirmishes with a quiet determination unknown to the whites.

A few days' pursuit of the Indians is generally enough to wear and tire out the ardor of the white man, as it is almost impossible to pursue Indians through their own country with wagons filled with supplies. It is also quite difficult for the cavalry horses to climb the barren, rugged mountain passes, which allows the Indians every advantage in their own mode of warfare. The weary soldiers return disheartened by often losing dear comrades and leaving them in a lonely grave on the plain. They are usually dissatisfied with only scattering their red foes.

But the weary savages rest during these intervals, often sending the friendly Indians, as they are called and believed to be, who are received in that character in the forts, and change it to a hostile one as soon as they reach the hills with new supplies of ammunition and food with which they then refresh themselves and further prosecute the war.

After the attack by General Sully was over, an Indian came to me with a letter to read, which he had taken from the pocket of a soldier who was killed by him. The letter stated that the topographical engineer had been killed, and that General Sully's men had caught the red devils, cut off their heads, and stuck them onto poles. The soldier had written a friendly and kind letter to his people, but, ere it was mailed, he was numbered with the dead.

X

Again My Life Is Spared

As soon as we were safe, and General Sully pursued us no longer, the warriors returned home, and a scene of terrible mourning over those killed ensued among the women. Their cries are terribly wild and distressing on such occasions, and the near relations of the deceased indulge in frantic expressions of grief that cannot be described. Sometimes the practice of cutting the flesh is carried to a horrible and barbarous extent. They inflict gashes on their bodies and limbs an inch in length. Some cut off all their hair, blacken their faces, and march through the village in procession, torturing their bodies to add vigor to their lamentations.

Hunger followed on the track of grief; all the food was gone and there was no game in that portion of the country. In our flight everything was scattered, and the country through which we passed for the following two weeks did not yield enough to arrest starvation. The Indians were terribly enraged and threatened me with death almost hourly.

I had so hoped for liberty when my friends were near; but alas! all my fond hopes were blasted. The Indians told me that the army was going in another direction.

The Indians seemed to have sustained a greater loss than I had been made aware of, which made them feel quite revengeful toward me. The next morning I could see that something unusual was about to happen. Notwithstanding the early hour, the sun scarcely appearing above the horizon, the principal chiefs and warriors were assembled in council, where, judging from the grave and reflective expression of their countenances, they were about to discuss some serious question.

I had reason for apprehension because of their unfriendly manner toward me, and feared for the penalty I might soon have to pay.

Soon they sent an Indian to me, who asked me if I was ready to die—to be burned at the stake. I told him whenever Wa-hon Tonka, the Great Spirit, was ready he would call for me, and then I would be ready and willing to go. He said that he had been sent from the council to warn me that it had become necessary to put me to death on account of my white brothers killing so many of their young men recently. He repeated that they were not cruel for the pleasure of being so; necessity is their first law, and he and the wise chiefs, faithful to their hatred for the white race, were in haste to satisfy their thirst for vengeance; and, further, that the interest of their nation required it.

As soon as all the chiefs were assembled around the council fire, the pipe-carrier entered the circle, holding in his hand the pipe already lighted. After bowing to the four cardinal points, he uttered a short prayer or invocation and then presented the pipe to the old chief, Ottawa, but retained the bowl in his hand. When all the chiefs and men had smoked, one after the other, the pipe-bearer emptied the ashes into the fire, saying, "Chiefs of the great Dakota nation, Wa-hon Tonka gives you wisdom so that whatever be your determination, it may be conformable to justice."

A moment of silence followed in which everyone appeared to be meditating seriously upon the words that had just been spoken. At length, one of the eldest of the chiefs, whose body was furrowed with the scars of innumerable wounds, and who enjoyed among his people a reputation for great wisdom, arose.

Said he, "The palefaces, our eternal persecutors, pursue and harass us without intermission, forcing us to abandon to them, one by one, our best hunting grounds, and we are compelled to seek a refuge in the depths of these Bad Lands like timid deer. Many of them even dare to come into the prairies which belong to us, to trap beaver and hunt elk and buffalo, which are our property. These undesirable creatures, the outcasts of their own people, rob and kill us when they can. Is it just that we should suffer these wrongs without complaining? Shall we allow ourselves to be massacred like timid Assiniboins,[1]

[1] A Siouan tribe in northeastern Montana and adjacent parts of Canada.

without seeking to avenge ourselves? Does not the law of the Dakotas say, 'Justice to our own nation and death to all palefaces?' Let my brothers say if that is just," pointing to the stake that was being prepared for me.

"Vengeance is always allowable," sententiously remarked Mahpeah (The Sky).

Then old chief Ottawa arose and said, "It is the undoubted right of the weak and oppressed; and yet it should be proportioned to the injury that was received. Then why should we put this young, innocent woman to death? Has she not always been kind to us, smiled upon us, and sang for us? Do not all our children love her as a tender sister? Why, then, should we put her to so cruel a death for the crimes of others, even if they are of her nation? Why should we punish an innocent one in place of the guilty?"

I looked to Heaven for mercy and protection, offering up those earnest prayers that are never offered in vain; and oh! how thankful I was when I knew their decision was to spare my life. Though terrible were my surroundings, life always became sweet to me, particularly when it seemed that I was about to part with it.

A terrible time ensued, and many dogs and horses died of starvation. Their bodies were eaten immediately; and the slow but constant march was kept up daily, in hope of finding game and better facilities for fish and fruit.

Many days in succession I tasted no food, save what I could gather on my way; a few rose leaves and blossoms was all I could find, except the grass I would gather and chew for nourishment. Fear, fatigue, and long-continued abstinence were wearing heavily on my already shattered frame. Women and children were crying for food; it was a painful sight to witness their sufferings with no means of alleviating them and no hope of relief save by traveling and hunting. We had no shelter save the canopy of heaven, and no alternative but to travel on, and at night lie down on the cold, damp ground for a resting place.

If I could but present to my readers a truthful picture of the Indian home at that time with all its sorrowful accompaniments! They are certainly engraved upon faithful memory, to last forever; but no touch of pen could give any semblance of the realities to another.

What exhibitions of their pride and passion I have seen. What ideas of their intelligence and humanity I have been compelled to form. What manifestations of their power and ability to govern had been thrust upon me. The treatment received was not such as to enhance in any way a woman's admiration for the so-called noble red man, but rather to make one pray to be delivered from their power.

Compelled to travel many days in succession and to experience the gnawings of hunger without mitigation, every day had its share of toil and fear. Yet while my temporal wants were thus poorly supplied, I was not wholly denied spiritual food. It was a blessed consolation that no earthly foe could interrupt my communion with the heavenly world. In those midnight, wakeful hours I was visited with many bright visions.

> *He walks with thee, that angel kind,*
> *And gently whispers, be resigned;*
> *Bear up, bear on, the end shall tell,*
> *The dear Lord ordereth all things well.*

XI

I Meet Another White Captive

IT WAS about this time that I had the sorrowful satisfaction of meeting with a victim of Indian cruelty, whose fate was even sadder than mine.

It was a part of my labor to carry water from the river upon whose banks we camped. When I wakened for that purpose, I silently arose and hurried out one morning before the day had yet dawned clearly, leaving the Indians still in their blankets and the village very quiet.

In the woods beyond I heard the retiring howl of the wolf. The shrill shriek of the bird of prey, as it was sweeping down upon the unburied carcass of some poor, murdered traveler, and the utter desolation of my life and its surroundings filled my heart with dread and gloom.

I was so reduced in strength and spirit that nothing but the fear of the scalping knife prodded my feet from task to task; and now, returning toward the tipi with my heavy bucket, I was startled to behold a fair-faced, beautiful young girl sitting there, dejected and worn, like myself, but bearing the marks of loveliness and refinement, despite her neglected covering.

Almost doubting my reason and sanity, for I had

become unsettled in my self-reliance, I feared to address her, but stood spellbound gazing upon her sad, brown eyes and drooping, pallid face.

The chief stood near the entrance of the tipi, enjoying the cool morning air and watching the interview with amusement. He offered me a book, which was one of the Willson's readers stolen from our wagons, and bade me show it to the stranger.[1]

I approached the girl, who instantly held out her hand and said: "What book is that?"

The sound of my own language, spoken by one of my own people, was too much for me, and I sank to the ground beside the stranger. While trying to clasp her in my arms, I became insensible.

A kindly squaw, who was aware of the situation, must have been touched by our helpless sorrow, for, when recovering, she began sprinkling my face with water from the bucket, and regarded me with a look of concern.

Of course, we realized that this chance interview would be too brief, and, perhaps, the last that we would be able to enjoy, and, while my companion covered her face and wept, I told my name and the main incidents of my capture. I dreaded to recall the possible fate of my Mary, lest I should rouse the terrible feelings I was trying to keep in subjection as my only hope of preserving reason.

[1] Marcus Willson (1813–1905) was the author of a number of popular primers and readers in the Harper's school and family series in the years after 1860.

The young girl responded to my confidence by giving her own story, which she related to me as follows:

"My name is Mary Boyeau; these people call me Madee.[2] I have been among them since the massacre in Minnesota and am now in my sixteenth year. My parents were of French descent, but we lived in the State of New York until my father, in pursuance of his peculiar passion for the life of a naturalist and a man of science, sold our eastern home and came to live on the shores of Spirit Lake, Minnesota.

"The Indians had watched about our place and regarded what they had seen of my father's chemical apparatus with awe and fear. Perhaps they suspected him of working evil charms in his laboratory or held his magnets, microscopes, and curiously-shaped tubes in superstitious aversion.

"I cannot tell; I only know that we were among the first victims of the massacre, and that all my family were murdered except myself, and, I fear, one younger sister."

"You fear!" said I. "Do you not hope that she escaped?"

[2] The editors have been unsuccessful in finding information about Mary Boyeau or her family. Fanny maintains here and in her petition to Congress that Mary was captured at the time of the Minnesota massacre in 1862, but the reference to Spirit Lake poses the possibility that she was taken in the earlier raid of 1857, though all accounts of that episode indicate that only four women were taken captive, of whom two were killed and two returned. None mention Mary Boyeau.

The poor girl shook her head. "From a life like mine, death is an escape," she said bitterly.

"Oh! it is fearful! and a sin to rush unbidden into God's presence, but I cannot live through another frightful winter.

"No, I must and will die if no relief comes to me. For a year these people regarded me as a child, and then a young man of their tribe gave a horse for me and carried me to his tipi as his wife."

"Do you love your husband?" I asked.

A look, bitter and revengeful, gleamed from her eyes.

"Love a savage, who bought me to be a drudge and slave!" she repeated. "No! I hate him as I hate all that belong to this fearful bondage. He has another wife and a child. Thank God!" she added with a shudder, "that I am not a mother!"

Misery and the consciousness of her own degraded life seemed to have made this poor young creature desperate; and, looking at her toil-worn hands and scarred arms, I saw the signs of abuse and cruelty; her feet, too, were bare and fearfully bruised and travel-marked.

"Does he ill treat you?" I inquired.

"His wife does," she answered. "I am forced to do different types of slavish chores, and when my strength fails, I am urged on by blows. Oh! I do so fearfully dread the chilling winters without proper food or clothing; and I long to lie down and die, if God's mercy will only permit me to escape from this hopeless imprisonment. I have nothing to expect now. I did once look forward to release, but that is all gone. I strove to go with the others, who were ransomed at Fort Pierre, and Mrs. Wright plead for me with all her heart; but the man who bought me would not give me up.

"Mr. Dupuy, a Frenchman, who brought a wagon for the redeemed women and children, did not offer enough for me; and when another man offered a horse my captor would not accept it.[3]

"There were many prisoners that I did not see in the village, but I am left alone. The Yanktons, who hold me, are friendly by pretense. They go to the agencies for supplies and annuities, but at heart they are bitterly hostile. They assert that if they did not murder and steal, the Father at Washington would forget them; so now they receive presents and supplies to keep them in check, which they delight in taking, and deceiving the officers as to their share in the outbreaks."

Her dread of soldiers was such that she had never

[3]This is probably Frederick Dupuis (or Dupree), a French-Canadian who was for many years a camp trader for the American Fur Company. It was not Dupuis, but Charles E. Galpin, of the firm of La Barge, Harkness and Company, who did the negotiating for several of the women captured by the Santee Sioux. Dupuis merely provided transportation from Fort La Framboise, just north of Pierre, for some of the ransomed captives as they headed back to Minnesota in November, 1862. John S. Gray, "The Santee Sioux and the Settlers at Lake Shetek," *Montana: The Magazine of Western History*, XXV (Winter, 1975), pp. 48–51.

attempted to escape, nor did she seem to think it possible to get away from her present life, so deep was the despair into which long-continued suffering had plunged her.

Sad as my condition was, I could not but pity poor Mary's worse fate. The unwilling wife of a brutal savage, and subject to all the petty malice of a scarcely less brutal squaw, there could be no gleam of sunshine in her future prospects. True, I was, like her, a captive torn from home and friends and subject to harsh treatment, but no such personal indignity had fallen to my lot.

When Mary was first taken, she saw many terrible things which she related to me, among which was the following:

One day the Indians entered into a house where they found a woman making bread. Her infant child lay in the cradle, unconscious of its fate. Snatching it from its little bed they thrust it into the heated oven, its screams torturing the wretched mother, who was then stabbed and cut in many pieces.

Taking the suffering little creature from the oven, they then dashed out its brains against the walls of the house.

One day on their journey they came to a narrow but deep stream of water. Some of the prisoners and nearly all of the Indians crossed on horseback while a few crossed on logs, which had been cut down by the beaver. A lady (by name of Mrs. Fletcher, I believe) who was in poor health, fell into the water with her heavy burden, unable, on account of her condition, to cross, and was shot by the Indians, her lifeless body soon disappearing from sight.[4] She also told me of a white man having been killed a few days previous, and a large sum of money taken from him, which would be exchanged for articles used among the Indians when they next visited the Red River or British Possessions. They went, she told me, two or three times a year, taking American horses, valuables, etc., which they had stolen from the whites, and exchanged them for ammunition, powder, arrow points, and provisions.

Before they reached the Missouri River they killed five of Mrs. Dooley's children,[5] one of which was left on the ground in a place where the distracted mother had to pass daily in carrying water from

[4]This is probably a reference to Mrs. Elizabeth Thatcher, a victim of the Spirit Lake assault of 1857, who was deliberately drowned and shot by her captors.

[5]Laura Duley and two of her daughters had been captured in the Santee attacks on the Lake Shetek settlements in southwest Minnesota in August, 1862. Her husband, William, was wounded but escaped; she had seen one of her children mortally wounded, another butchered by a squaw with a knife and she herself suffered a wound in the heel and later had a miscarriage as a result of mistreatment by her captors. In November, thanks to Charles Galpin and other traders, she and her daughters were ransomed. It was her husband, Captain William J. Duley, who was chosen to cut the rope that simultaneously sprang the traps under the thirty-eight Santee Sioux hanged on December 26, 1882. John S. Gray, "The Santee Sioux and the Settlers at Lake Shetek," *Montana: The Magazine of Western History*, XXV (Winter, 1975), pp. 43, 46–47, 51, 54.

the river; and when they left the camp the body still remained unburied. So terrible were the sufferings of this heartbroken mother that, when she arrived in safety back among the whites, her reason soon became dethroned, and I was told that she was sent to the lunatic asylum, where her distracted husband soon followed.

Mary wished that we might be together, but knew that it would be useless to ask, as it would not be granted. I gave her my book and half of my pencil, which she was glad to receive. I wrote her name in the book, together with mine, encouraging her with kind words and hope. She could read and write English, and understood the Indian language.

The book had been taken from our wagon and I had endeavored to teach the Indians from it. It made the Indians very angry to have me part with it. For hours I had sat with the book in my hands, showing them the pictures and explaining their meaning which interested them greatly, and which helped pass away and relieve the monotony of the days of captivity which I was enduring. Moreover, it inspired them with a degree of respect and veneration for me when engaged in the task, which was not only pleasant but a great comfort. It was by this means they discovered my usefulness in writing letters and reading for them.

I found them apt pupils, willing to learn, and they learned easily and rapidly. Their memory is very retentive—unusually good.

XII

Despair and Delirium

ONE DAY as I was pursuing what seemed to me an endless journey, an Indian rode up beside me, whom I did not remember to have seen before.

At his saddle hung a bright and well-known little shawl, and onto the other side was suspended a child's scalp of long, fair hair.

As my eyes rested on the frightful sight, I trembled in my saddle and grasped the air for support. A blood-red cloud seemed to come between me and the outer world, and I realized that innocent victim's dying agonies.

The torture was too great to be endured, and a merciful insensibility quickly interposed between me and madness.

I dropped from the saddle as if dead and rolled upon the ground at the horse's feet.

When I recovered, I found myself clinging to a squaw who was vainly attempting to extricate herself from my clutches.

With returning consciousness, I raised my eyes to the fearful sight that had almost deprived me of reason; it was gone.

The Indian had suspected the cause of my emotion and removed it out of sight.

They placed me in the saddle once more, and not being able to control the horrible misery I felt, I protested wildly against their touch, imploring them to kill me, and frantically inviting the death I had before feared and avoided.

When the Indians camped, I had not the power or reason to seek my own tent, but fell down in the sun, where the chief found me lying. He had been out at the head of a scouting party and knew nothing of my sufferings.

Instantly approaching me, he inquired who had misused me. I replied, "No one. I want to see my dear mother, my poor mother who loves me and pines for her unhappy child."

I had found by experience that the only grief with which this red nation had any sympathy was the sorrow one might feel for a separation from a mother, and even the chief seemed to recognize the propriety of such emotion.

On this account I feigned to be grieving solely for my dear widowed mother, and accordingly was treated with more consideration than I had dared to expect.

Leaving me for several moments, he returned, bringing me some ripe wild plums, which were deliciously cooling to my fever-parched lips.

Hunger and thirst, sorrow and fear, with unusual fatigue and labor had weakened me in mind and body, so that, after trying to realize the frightful vision that had almost deprived me of my senses, I began to waver in my knowledge of it, and half determined that it was a hideous phantom like many another that had tortured my lonely hours.

I tried to dismiss the awful dream from remembrance, particularly as the days that followed found me ill and delirious, and it was some time before I was able to recall events clearly.

About this time another battle had begun and many were sinking under the united misery of hunger and fatigue. The camp was gloomy and hopeless in the extreme.

The Indians had discovered my skill in dressing wounds, and I was called immediately to the relief of the wounded brought into camp.

The fight lasted three days, and from the immoderate lamentations I supposed many had fallen, but could form no idea of the loss.

Except when encamped for rest, the tribe pursued their wanderings rather constantly; sometimes flying before the enemy, at others endeavoring to elude them.

I kept the record of time, as it passed with the savages, as well as I was able, and with the exception of a few days lost during temporary delirium and fever at two separate times, and which I endeavored to supply by careful inquiry, I missed no count of the rising or setting sun, and knew dates almost as well as if I were in the heart of civilization.

One very hot day a dark cloud seemed suddenly to pass before the sun and threaten a great storm.

The wind rose and the cloud became still darker until the light of day was almost obscured.

A few raindrops sprinkled the earth and then, in a heavy, blinding, and apparently inexhaustible shower, a countless swarm of grasshoppers covered everything and rendered the air almost black by their descent.

It is impossible to convey an idea of their extent; they seemed to rival Pharaoh's locusts in number, and no doubt would have done damage to the food of the savages had they not fallen victims themselves to their keen appetites.

To catch them, large holes are dug in the ground which are heated by fires. Into these apertures the insects are then driven, and, the fires having been removed, the heated earth bakes them.

They are considered good food, and were greedily devoured by the famishing Sioux. Although the grasshoppers only remained two days and went as suddenly as they had come, the Indians seemed refreshed by feasting on such small game and continued to move forward.

Halting one day to rest beside good water, I busily engaged myself in the chief's tipi or lodge. I had grown so weak that motion of any kind was exhausting to me and I could scarcely walk. I felt that I must soon die of starvation and sorrow; life had ceased to be dear to me.

Mechanically I tried to fulfill my tasks, so as to secure the continued protection of the old squaw who, when not incensed by passion, was not devoid of kindness.

My strength failed me, and I could no longer carry on. I almost fell as I tried to move around. This met with disapprobation, and, better fed than myself, she could not sympathize with my want of strength. She became cross and left the lodge, threatening me with her vengeance.

Presently an Indian woman who pitied me ran into the tipi in great haste, saying that her husband had some deer meat. She had cooked it for a feast and begged me to share it. As she spoke, she drew me toward her tent, and being hungry and fainting I readily followed.

The chief saw us go and, not disdaining a good dinner, followed along. The old squaw came flying into the lodge like an enraged fury, flourishing her knife, and vowing she would kill me.

I arose immediately and fled, the squaw pursuing me. The chief attempted to interfere, but her rage was too great. He struck her, at which she sprang like an infuriated tiger upon him, stabbing him in several places.

Her brother, who at a short distance beheld the fray, and deeming me the cause, fired six shots determining to kill me. One of these shots lodged in the arm of the chief, breaking it near the shoulder. I then ran until I reached the outskirts of the village where I was captured by a party who saw me running but who knew not the cause.

Thinking that I was endeavoring to escape, they dragged me into the tent, brandishing their tomahawks and threatening vengeance.

After the lapse of half an hour, several squaws came and took me back to the lodge of the chief, who was waiting for me before his wounds could be dressed. He was very weak from loss of blood.

I never saw the wife of the chief afterward.

Indian surgery is coarse and rude in its details. A doctor of the tribe had pierced the arm of the chief with a long knife, probing in search of the ball it had received, and the wound thus enlarged had to be healed.

As soon as I was able to stand, I was required to go and wait on the disabled chief. I found his three sisters with him, and with these I continued to live in companionship.

One of them had been married at the fort to a white man, whom she had left at Laramie when his prior wife arrived.

She told me that they were esteemed friendly and had often received supplies from the fort, although at heart they would be eternally the enemy of the white man.

"But will they not suspect you?" asked I. "They will surely discover your deceit and punish you some day."

She laughed derisively. "Our prisoners don't escape to tell tales," she replied. "Dead people don't talk. We claim friendship and they cannot prove that we don't feel it. Besides, all white soldiers are cowards."

Shudderingly, I turned away from this enemy of my race and prepared to wait on my captor, whose superstitious belief in the healing power of a white woman's touch led him to desire her services.

The wounds of the chief were severe, and the suppuration profuse. It was my task to bathe and dress the wounds and prepare his food.

Hunting and fishing being now out of the question for him, he had sent his wives to work for themselves while keeping the sisters and myself to attend him.

War with our soldiers seemed to have decreased the power of the chief to a great extent. As he lay ill, he probably meditated on some plan of strengthening his forces, and finally concluded to send an offer of marriage to the daughter of the war chief of another band.

As General Sully's destructive attack had deprived him all ready offerings, he availed himself of my shoes, which happened to be particularly good, and, reducing me to moccasins, sent them as a gift to the expected bride.

She evidently received them graciously for she came to his lodge almost every day to visit him and sat chatting at his side, to his apparent satisfaction.

The pleasure of this new matrimonial acquisition on the part of the chief had a trying effect on me on account of my limited wardrobe, because as the betrothed continued in favor, the chief evinced it by giving her articles of my clothing.

An Indian woman had given me a red silk sash, the kind the officers wear. The chief unceremoniously cut it in half, leaving me one half, while the coquettish squaw received the rest.

An Indian husband's power is absolute even to death. No woman can have more than one husband, but an Indian man can have as many wives as he chooses.

The marriage of the chief was to be celebrated with all due ceremony when his arm got well, but his arm never recovered. Mr. Clemens,[1] the interpreter, tells me (in my late interview with him) that he still remains crippled and unable to carry out any of his murderous intentions to go with his anticipated wicked designs.

He is now living in several of the forts along the Missouri River, gladly claiming support from the Government.

[1]This was probably Basil Clement, a St. Louisan who had been a part of the Upper Missouri fur trade since 1840, often in charge of trading with the Indians for the American Fur Company. Fluent in the Sioux dialects, Clement had served as guide and interpreter for Harney, then Sully in 1864, plus numerous army survey parties in the Dakotas, Wyoming and Montana.

XIII

Hope of Rescue

BEFORE the Indians departed this campground, there arrived among us an Indian known as Porcupine. He was well dressed and mounted on a fine horse. He brought with him presents and valuables that insured him a cordial reception.

After he had been a few days in the village, he gave me a letter from Captain Marshall[1] of the Eleventh Ohio Cavalry which detailed the unsuccessful attempts that had been made to rescue me, and also stated that this friendly Indian had undertaken to bring me back for which he would be rewarded.

The letter further said that he had already received a horse along with necessary provisions for the journey, and had left his three wives, with thirteen others, at the fort as hostages.

My feelings on reading this letter were indescribable. My heart leaped with unaccustomed hope at this evidence of the efforts of my white friends on my behalf; but the next instant despair succeeded this gleam of happy anticipation for I knew this faithless messenger would not keep his promise,

[1]Captain Levi E. Marshall. Camp Marshall, at La Bonte on the Overland Trail west of Fort Laramie, was named after him in 1864.

since he had joined the Sioux immediately after his arrival in a battle against the whites.

My fears were not wholly unfounded. Porcupine prepared to go back to the fort without me, disregarding my earnest prayers and entreaties.

The chief found me useful and determined to keep me. He believed that a woman who had seen so much of their deceitfulness and cruelty could do them injury at the fort, and might prevent their receiving annuities.

Porcupine said he would report me to be dead or impossible to find, and I could not prevail upon him to do anything to the contrary.

When reminded of the possible vengeance of the soldiers on his wives, whom they had threatened to kill if he did not bring me back, he laughed.

"The white soldiers are cowards," he answered. "They never kill women, and I will deceive them as I have done before."

Saying this, he took his departure; nor could my most urgent entreaties induce the chief to yield his consent and allow me to send a written message to my friends, or through any other means assure them of my existence.

All hope of rescue departed and sadly I turned again to the wearisome drudgery of my captive life.

The young betrothed bride of the old chief was very gracious to me. On one occasion she invited me to join her in a walk. The day was cool and the air temptingly balmy.

"Down there," she said, pointing to a deep ravine. "Come and walk there; it is cool and shady."

I looked in the direction indicated and then at the Indian girl, who became very mysterious in her manner as she whispered:

"There are white people down there."

"How far?" I asked, eagerly.

"About fifty miles," she answered. "They have great guns and men dressed in many buttons. Their wagons are drawn by horses with long ears."

A fort, thought I, but remembering the treacherous nature of the people I was among, I repressed every sign of emotion and tried to look indifferent.

"Should you like to see them?" questioned Egosegalonicha, as she was called.

"They are strangers to me," I said quietly; "I do not know them."

"Are you sorry to live with us?"

"You do not have such bread as I would like to eat," I replied cautiously.

"And are you dissatisfied with our home?"

"You have some meat now; it is better than that at the other camping ground. There we had no food and I suffered."

"But your eyes are swollen and red," she hinted; "you do not weep for bread."

These questions made me suspicious, and I tried to evade the young squaw, but in vain.

"Just see how green that wood is," I said, affecting not to hear her.

Porcupine, a Sioux Warrior
Courtesy Denver Public Library

"But you do not say you are content," she repeated. "Will you stay here always, willingly?"

"Come and listen to the birds," said I, drawing my companion toward the grove.

I did not trust her, and feared to utter a single word lest it might be used against me with the chief.

I did not err in the design of Egosegalonicha, for when we returned to the lodge, I overheard her relating to the chief the amusement she had enjoyed in lying to the white woman, repeating what she had told me about the fort and inventing entreaties which I had used, urging her to allow me to fly to my white friends and leave the Indians forever.

Instantly I resolved to take advantage of the affair as a joke, and, approaching the chief with respectful pleasantry, begged to reverse the story.

It was the squaw who had implored me to go with her to the white man's fort, I said, and find her a white warrior for a husband; but, true to my faith with the Indians, I refused.

The wily Egosegalonicha, thus finding her weapons turned against herself, appeared confused and suddenly left the tent, at which the old chief smiled grimly.

Slander, like a vile serpent, coils itself around these Indian women; and, as with our fair sisters in a civilized society, when reality fails, invention is called in to supplant the defect. They find scandal delightful and prove by it their claim to some of the refined conventionalities of civilized life.

Porcupine had spread the news throughout the village that a large reward had been offered for the white woman, consequently I was sought after, the motive being to gain the reward.

One day an Indian, whom I had seen in different places and whose wife I had known, made signs intimating a desire for my escape, and assuring me of his help to return to my people.

I listened to his plans and although I knew my position to be one of great peril, I felt that my life was of such little value that any opportunity, however slight, was as a star in the distance, and escape should be attempted, even at a risk.

We conversed as well as we could several times and finally arrangements were made. At night, he was to make a slight scratching noise as a sign at the tipi where I was. The night came, but I was singing to the people and could not get away. Another time we had visitors in the lodge, and I would be missed. The next night I arose from my robe and went out into the darkness. Seeing my intended rescuer at a short distance, I approached and followed him. We ran hastily out of the village about a mile, where we were to be joined by the squaw who had helped make the arrangements and was favorable to the plan for my escape, but she was not there. White Tipi (that was the Indian's name) looked hastily around, and, seeing no one, darted away without a word of explanation. Why the Indian acted thus I never knew. It was a strange proceeding.

Fear lent me wings and I flew, rather than ran, back to my tipi, where, exhausted and discouraged, I dropped on the ground and feigned slumber for the inmates were already aroused, having just discovered my absence. Finding me apparently asleep, they lifted me up, and taking me into the tent, laid me upon my own robe.

The next evening White Tipi sent for me to come and feast at his lodge. I was well and hospitably entertained, but not a sign was given of the adventure of the previous night. Then when the pipe was passed, he requested it to be touched to my lips, then offered it to the Great Spirit thus signifying his friendship for me.

In this month the Indians captured a white man, who was hunting on the prairie. After carrying him far away from the haunts of white men, they tied him hand and foot, after divesting him of all clothing, and left him to starve. He was never heard of afterward.

There were twin children in one of the lodges, one of which sickened and died, and in the evening was buried. The surviving child was placed upon the scaffold by the corpse and there remained all night, its crying and moaning almost breaking my heart. I inquired why they did this. The reply was, to cause the mate to mourn. The mother was on one of the neighboring hills wailing and weeping, as is the custom among them. Nearly every night there were women in the hills, wailing for their dead.

XIV

Indian Camp Scenes

About the first of October, the Indians were on the move as usual, and by some means I became separated from the family I was with and was lost. I looked around for them, but their familiar faces were not to be seen. Strangers gazed upon me, and although I asked them to assist me in finding the people of my own tipi, they paid no attention to my trouble and refused to do anything for me.

Never shall I forget the sadness I felt as evening approached and we encamped for the night in a lonely valley, after a wearisome day's journey.

Along one side stood a strip of timber with a small stream beside it. Hungry, weary, and lost to my people, with no place to lay my head, and after a fruitless search for the family, I was more desolate than ever. Even Keoku, or "Yellow Bird," the Indian girl who had been given to me, was not with me that day, making it still more lonely.

I sat down and held my pony. It was autumn and the forest wore the last glory of its gorgeous coloring. Already the leaves lay along the paths, like a rich carpet of variegated colors. The winds caught a deeper tone, mournful as the tones of an aeolian harp, but the air was balmy, and the sunlight lay warm and pleasant, as one finds in midsummer, over the beautiful valley now occupied with numberless camps of tentless Indians. It seemed as if the soft autumn weather was, to the last moment, unwilling to yield the last traces of beauty to the chilled embraces of stern winter, and I thought of the luxuries and comforts of my home. I looked back on the past with tears of sorrow and regret; my heart was overburdened with grief and I prayed to die. The future looked like a dark cloud approaching, for the dread of the desolation of winter was appalling to me.

While I was meditating on days of the past and contemplating the future, Keoku came upon me and was delighted to find the object of her search.

They had been looking for me and did not know where I had gone. Since they had become quite worried about me, she said she was glad she had found me. I was as pleased as she appeared to be and rejoiced to join them.

One has no idea of the extent of an Indian village or of the number of its inhabitants. It would seem strange to some that I should ever get lost when among them, but, like a large city, one may be separated from their companions, and in a few moments be lost.

The Indians all knew the "white woman," yet I knew but few, and consequently when among strangers, I felt utterly friendless.

The experience of those days of gloom and sadness seem like a fearful dream now that my life is once again with civilized people and enjoying the blessings that I was there deprived of.

Some twenty-five years ago an emigrant train, enroute to California arrived in the neighborhood of the crossing of the North Platte and cholera broke out among the travelers. Everyone died with the exception of one little girl.

The Indian "Black Bear," while hunting, came to the wagons, now a morgue, and finding the father of the girl dying with cholera, took the child in his arms. The dying parent begged him to carry his little one to his home in the East, assuring him of an abundant reward by the child's friends, in addition to the gold he gave him. These facts I determined from a letter which had been given to Black Bear by the dying father, and which had been carefully preserved by the daughter.

Instead of doing as was desired, Black Bear took the money, child, and everything valuable in the train to his own home among the hills, and there educated the little one with habits of savage life.

She forgot her own language, her name, and everything about her past life, but she knew that she was white. Her infancy and girlhood were, therefore, passed in utter ignorance of the modes of life of her own people. Contented and happy, she remained among them, verifying the old adage that "habit is second nature." When she was of marriageable age, Black Bear took her for his wife, and they had a child, a boy.

Shortly after I went into the village, I became acquainted with this white woman and immediately we were sincere friends, although no confidants as I dared not trust her. It was very natural and pleasant to know her as she was white, and although she was an Indian in tastes and habits, she was my sister and belonged to my race. There was a sympathetic chord between us, and it was a relief to be with her.

On the occasion of my first visit with her, Black Bear suggested the idea that white women always drank tea together, so she made us a cup of herb tea which we drank in company.

I endeavored to enlighten her, and to do her all the good I could; told her of the white people, and of their kindness and Christianity, trying to impress her with the superiority of the white race, all of which she listened to with great interest.

I was the only white woman she had seen, for whenever they neared any fort she was always kept out of sight.

She seemed to enjoy painting herself and dressing for the dances as well as the squaws, and was happy and contented with Indian surroundings, for she knew no difference.

I know not what has become of her, for I have never heard; neither can I remember the name of her father.

A fourteen-year-old boy named Charles Sylvester from Quincy, Illinois was stolen when seven years of age. One day I saw him playing with the Indian boys in the village and, discovering immediately that he was a white boy, I flew to his side and tried to clasp him in my arms. In my joy I exclaimed, "Oh! I know you are a white boy! Speak to me, and tell me who you are and where you come from!" He also had forgotten his name and parentage, but knew that he was white.

When I spoke to him, the boys began to plague and tease him, and he refused to speak to me, running away every time I approached him.

About a year after, when this boy was out hunting, he killed a comrade by accident, and he dared not return to the village; so he escaped on his pony to the white people. On his way to the States, he called at a house where they knew what tribe he belonged to, and they questioned him as to whether he had seen a white woman in the village. He replied in the affirmative and from a bundle of pictures given him he picked mine out saying, "That is the white woman whom I saw."

After a while, being discontented with his own people, he returned to his adopted friends on the North Platte and became an interpreter and trader. He still remains there doing business at various posts.

When the Indians went to obtain their annuities, they transferred me to the Unkpapas, leaving me in the charge of a young couple and an old Indian who had four wives. The old one had been very brave, it was said, for he had endured the trial which proves the successful warrior. He was one of those who "looked at the sun" without failing in heart or strength.

This custom is as follows: The one who undergoes this operation is nearly naked, and is suspended from the upper end of a pole by a cord which is tied to some splints which run through the flesh of both breasts. The weight of his body is hung from it, yet the feet are still barely touching the ground. In his left hand he holds his favorite bow, and in his right, with a firm hold, his medicine bag.

A great crowd usually assembles, sympathizing with and encouraging him, but he still continues to hang and "look at the sun," without paying the least attention to anyone about him. The mystery men beat their drums, and shake their rattles, and sing as loud as they can yell so as to strengthen his heart to look at the sun from its rising until its setting, at which time, if his heart and strength have not failed him, he is "cut down," receives a liberal donation of presents which are piled before him during the day, and also the name and style of a doctor or medicine man, which lasts him, and ensures him respect through life. It is considered a test of bravery. Superstition seems to have full sway among the Indians—just as much as in heathen lands beyond the sea, where the Burmah mother casts her child to the crocodile in order to please the Great Spirit.

Many of these Indians were from Minnesota, and

were of the group that escaped justice two years before, after committing indiscriminate slaughter of men, women, and children. One day I was sent for by one of them, and when seated in his lodge, he gave me a letter to read, which was purported to have been written by General Sibley, as follows:

This Indian, after taking part in the present outbreak of the Indians against the white settlers and missionaries, being sick, and not able to keep up with his friends in their flight, we give you the offerings of friendship, food, and clothing. You are in our power, but we won't harm you. Go to your people and gladden their hearts. Lay down your weapons and fight the white men no more. We will do you good and not evil. Take this letter; in it we have spoken. Depart in peace, and ever more be a friend to the white people, and you will be more happy.

H. H. SIBLEY,[1]
Brig. Gen., Commanding Expedition

Instinctively I looked up into his face, and said: "Do you truly intend to keep your promise?" He laughed derisively at the idea of an Indian brave abandoning his profession. He told of many instances of outrageous cruelties by his band in their

[1] A veteran fur trader with the American Fur Company, Henry Hastings Sibley (1811–91) built his home across the Minnesota River at Fort Snelling, was elected Minnesota delegate to Washington, and became the state's first governor. During the Sioux uprising, Sibley was put in command of the state militia and was subsequently named brigadier general by President Lincoln, and in 1863–64 was in charge of the military expeditions against the Sioux in Dakota.

marauding and murderous attacks upon wagon trains and frontier settlers; and, further, to assure me of his bravery, he showed me a puzzle or game he had made from the finger bones of some of the victims that had fallen beneath his own tomahawk. The bones had been freed from the flesh by boiling, and, being placed upon a string, were used for playing some kind of Indian game. This is but one of the heathenish acts of these Indians.

The Indians take pleasure in recounting their exploits, and, savage-like, dwell with much satisfaction upon the number of scalps they have taken from their white enemies. They would be greatly amused at the shuddering horror manifested when, to irritate me, they would tauntingly portray the dying agonies of white men, women, and children who had fallen into their hands; and particularly would the effect of their description of the murder of little Mary afford them satisfaction. I feel, now, that I must have been convinced of her death, yet I could not then help hoping that she had escaped.

These exploits and incidents are generally related by the Indians when in camp having nothing to do. The great lazy brutes would sit by the hour making caricatures of white soldiers, representing them in various ways, and always as cowards and inferior beings; sometimes as in combat, but always at their mercy. This was frequently done, apparently to annoy me, and one time, losing patience, I snatched a rude drawing from the hands of an Indian, who was holding it up to my view, and tore it in two, clasping the part that represented the white soldier to my heart, and throwing the other in the fire. Then, looking up, I told them the white soldiers were dear to me; that they were my friends and I loved them. I said they were friends to the Indians and did not want to harm them. I expressed myself in the strongest manner by words and signs.

Never did I see a more enraged set of men. They assailed me with burning firebrands, burning me severely. They heated the points of their arrows, and burned and threatened me sorely.

I told them I meant no harm to them. That it was ridiculous, their getting angry at my burning a bit of paper. I promised I would make them some pictures, and at last I pacified them. They were much like children in this respect—easily offended, but very difficult to please.

I was constantly annoyed, worried, and terrified by their peculiar conduct—their transition from laughing and fun to anger, and even rage. I knew not how to get along with them. One moment they would seem friendly and kind; the next, if any act of mine displeased them, their faces were instantly changed, and they displayed their hatred or anger in unmeasured language or conduct—children one hour, fiends the next. I always tried to please them and was as cheerful as I could be under the circumstances, for my own sake.

One day I was called to see a man who lay in his

tipi in great suffering. His wasted face was darkened by fever, and his brilliantly restless eyes rolled anxiously, as if in search of relief from pain. He was reduced to a skeleton, and had endured tortures from the suppuration of an old wound in the knee.

He greeted me with the "How! How!" of Indian politeness, and, in answer to my inquiry why he came to suffer so, replied:

"I go to fight white man. He take away land and chase game away; then he take away our squaws. He take away my best squaw."

Here his voice choked and he displayed much emotion.

Pitying his misery, I endeavored to aid him, and rendered him all the assistance in my power, but death was then upon him.

The medicine man was with him also, practicing his incantations.

We were so constantly traveling, it wearied me beyond expression. The day after the Indian's burial, we were again on the move.

XV

My First Contact with the Soldiers

ONE OF the occupations given me, while resting in the villages between war times, was to prepare the bark of a red willow called *killikinnick*, as a substitute for tobacco.

Furthermore, they discovered that I could sing, and groups of idle warriors would gather around me before the tent, urging me to sing as I worked. A dreary, dreary task! chanting to please my savage companions while I rubbed and prepared the bark of willow, my heart ready to burst with grief.

On the fifth of September they went to battle and surprised a portion of Captain Fisk's men who were escorting an emigrant train.[1] Fourteen soldiers were killed, and two wagons loaded with whisky, wines, and valuable articles were taken.

[1] James Liberty Fisk (1835–1902), born within sound of Niagara Falls, moved progressively west, gaining valuable experience in frontier journalism along the way. Settling in Minnesota in 1857, he became associated with the Dakota Land Company and promoted the "Northern Overland Route" to the gold fields of Montana. Moreover, he urged that emigrants along the route be given military protection. The War Department authorized army escorts in 1862, and in 1864, when Fanny Kelly's path crossed his, Captain Fisk was escorting his third party of emigrants to the gold fields. Later, he helped a brother edit the *Helena Herald*.

Among the articles brought into camp were a number of pickles in glass jars, which the Indians tasted. The result was comical in the extreme, for there is nothing that an Indian abhors more than a strong acid. The faces they made can be imagined but not described. Thinking that they might be improved by cooking, they placed the jars in the fire, where, of course, they exploded, very much to the Indians' disgust for the "white man's kettles."

I could hear the firing plainly, and when they returned that night in triumph, bringing with them many plundered items, they committed every description of extravagant demonstration. In the wild orgies which followed, they mocked and groaned in imitation of the dying, and went through a horrid mimicry of the butchery they had perpetrated.

They determined to go out again and capture a quantity of horses corralled in the neighborhood, and sweep the train and soldiers with wholesale massacre; but they feared the white man's cannon, and deliberated on means of surprising by ambush, which is their only idea of warfare.

Indians are not truly brave, though they are vain of the name of courage. Cunning, stealth, strategy, and deceit are the weapons they use in attack.

They endure pain because they are taught from infancy that it is cowardly to flinch, but they will never stand to fight if they can strike secretly and quickly escape.

Fearing the cannon, yet impatient for the spoil,

the Indians waited for three days for the train to move on and leave them free to attack.

For two days I implored and begged on my knees to be allowed to go with them, but to no avail. At last, I succeeded in inducing them to allow me to write, as they knew I understood the nature of correspondence. They procured for me the necessary appliances and dictated a letter to Captain Fisk, assuring him the Indians were weary of fighting and advising him to go on in peace and safety.

Knowing their malicious designs, I set myself to work to circumvent them; and although the wily chief counted every word he dictated as they were marked on paper, I contrived, by joining them together and condensing the information I gave, to warn the officer of the perfidious intentions of the savages, and tell him briefly of my helpless and unhappy captivity.

The letter was once again carefully examined by the chief, and the number of its apparent words recounted.

At length, appearing satisfied with its contents, he had it carried to a hill in sight of the soldier's camp, and stuck on a pole.

After a reasonable interval the reply arrived, and again my ingenuity was tasked to read the answer corresponding with the number of words that would not condemn me.

The captain's real statement was that he distrusted all among the savages, and had great reason to.

Upon reading Captain Fisk's words, my awakened hopes were severely crushed and my emotion overcame me.

Having told the Indians that the captain doubted their friendliness, and explaining the contents of the letter as I thought best, the next day I was entrusted with the task of writing again to solemnly assure the soldiers of the faith and friendship the Indians professed.

Again I managed to communicate with them, and this time begged them to use their field glasses, and that I would find an excuse for standing on the hills in the afternoon, that they might see for themselves that I was what I represented myself to be—a white woman held in bondage.

The opportunity I desired was gained, and to my great delight I had a chance of standing so as to be seen by the men in the soldier's camp.

I had given my own name in every communication. As soon as the soldiers saw that it truly was a woman of their own race, and that I was in the power of their enemies, the excitement of their feelings became so great that they desired immediately to rush to my rescue.

A gentleman belonging to the train generously offered eight hundred dollars for my ransom, which was all the money he had, and the noble, manly feeling displayed in my behalf did honor to those who felt it. There was not a man in the train who was not willing to sacrifice all he had for my rescue.

Captain James L. Fisk

Courtesy State Historical Society of North Dakota

143

Captain Fisk restrained all hasty demonstrations, and even went so far as to say that the first man who moved in the direction of the Indian camp should be shot immediately, his experience enabling him to know that a move of that kind would result fatally to them and to the captive.

It was during this time that the Indians found a box of crackers saturated with water, and shortly after eating them, sickened and died.

I afterward learned that some persons with the train who had suffered the loss of dear relatives and friends in the Minnesota massacre, and who had lost their all, had poisoned the crackers with strychnine and left them on one of their camping grounds without the captain's knowledge.[2]

The Indians told me afterward that many more had died from eating bad bread than from bullets during the whole summer campaign.

Captain Fisk deserves great credit for his daring and courage, with his meager supply of men against so large an army of red men.

After the assurance of my presence among them, Captain Fisk proceeded to treat quietly with the

[2]Some twenty-five Indians reportedly died from eating the poisoned hardtack left by emigrants. Fisk denied any part in the affair but wrote that "unwarlike means of destruction" probably saved the train. Quoting Macbeth, he continued, "and find after it was done, that it *was* done, I *was glad 'twas well done!*" These intemperate remarks included in his official report were suppressed by the War Department for nearly a hundred years. White, ed. *Ho! For the Gold Fields*, pp. 117, 150–51.

savages on the subject of a ransom, offering to deliver into their village three wagonloads of stores as a price for their prisoner.

To this the deceitful creatures readily pretended to agree, while I, the tortured captive, who could understand their tongue, heard them making fun of the credulity of white soldiers who did not doubt their promises.

I had the use of a field glass from the Indians, and with it I saw my white friends, which almost made me wild with excited hope.

Knowing what the Indians were planning, and dreading that the messengers should be killed, as I knew they would be if they came to the village, I wrote to Captain Fisk about the futility of ransoming me in that way, and warned him of the treachery intended against his messengers.

No tongue can tell or pen describe those terrible days, when, seemingly lost to hope and surrounded by drunken Indians, my life was in constant danger.

Nights of horrible revelry passed, when, forlorn and despairing, I lay listening, only half consciously, to the savage mirth and wild exultation.

To no overtures would the Indians listen, declaring I could not be purchased at any price since they were determined not to part with me. Captain Fisk and his companions were sadly disappointed in not obtaining my release, and, after a hopeless attempt, he made known the fact of my being a prisoner, spreading the news far and wide.

His expeditions across the plains had always been successful, and the Indians, knowing him to be very brave, gave him the name of the "Great Chief Who Knows No Fear," and he richly deserves the appellation, for the expeditions he led were attended with great danger. The reports of his various expeditions have been published by the Government and are very interesting.

In September the rains were very frequent, sometimes continuing for days. This may not seem serious to those who have always been accustomed to a dwelling and a good bed, but to me, who had no shelter and whose shrinking form was exposed to the pitiless storm, and nought but the cold ground to lie upon, bringing the pains and distress of rheumatism, it was a calamity difficult to bear. I often prayed fervently to God to give me sweet release in a flight to the land where there are no storms.

Soon the winter would be upon us, and the cold, and sleet, and stormy weather would be more difficult to bear. Would I be so fortunate, would Heaven be so gracious as to place me into circumstances where the wintry winds could not chill or make me suffer! When I thought of what the future held my heart became faint, for hope was lessening as winter approached!

XVI

Reflections

WELL DO I remember my thoughts and feelings when first I beheld the mighty and beautiful prairie of Cannonball River.[1] With what singular emotions I beheld it for the first time! I could compare it to nothing but a vast sea, changed suddenly to earth, with all its heaving, rolling billows. Thousands of acres lay spread before me like a mighty ocean, bounded by nothing but the deep blue sky. What a magnificent sight—a sight that made my soul expand with lofty thought and its frail tenement sink into utter nothingness before it! Well do I remember my sad thoughts and the turning of my mind upon the past as I stood alone upon a slight rise of ground and overlooked miles upon miles of the most lovely, the most sublime scene I had ever beheld. Wave upon wave of land stretched away on every hand, covered with beautiful green grass and the blooming wild flowers of the prairie. Occasionally I caught glimpses of wild animals, while flocks of birds of various kinds and beautiful plumage skimming over the surface here and there, alighting

[1] The Cannonball River flows across southwestern North Dakota and joins the Missouri thirty miles or so south of Bismarck.

147

or darting upward from the earth, added life and beauty and variety to this most enchanting scene.

It had been a beautiful day and the sun was now just burying himself in the far-off ocean of blue. His golden rays were streaming along the surface of the waving grass and tinging it with a delightful hue. Occasionally an elevated point caught and reflected his rays to the one I was standing on, and it would catch, for a moment, his fading rays and glow like a ball of fire. Slowly he started his diurnal farewell, as if loath to quit a scene so lovely, and at last hid himself from my view beyond the horizon.

I stood and marked every change with that poetical feeling of pleasant sadness which a beautiful sunset rarely fails to awaken in the breast of the lover of nature. I noted every change that was going on, yet my thoughts were far, far away. I thought of the hundreds of miles that separated me from the friends that I loved. I was recalling the delight with which I had, when a little girl, viewed the farewell scenes of day from so many romantic hills, and lakes, and rivers, rich meadows, mountain gorge and precipice, and the quiet hamlets of my dear native land so far away. I fancied I could see my mother move to the door with a slow step and heavy heart, and gaze, with yearning affection, toward the broad, the mighty West and sigh, wondering what had become of her lost child.

I thought, and grew more sad as I thought, until tears filled my eyes.

Mother! what a world of affection is comprised in that single word; how little do we in the giddy round of youthful pleasure and folly heed her wise counsels. How lightly do we look upon that zealous care with which she guides our otherwise erring feet, and watches with feelings which none but a mother can know the gradual expansion of our youth to the riper years of discretion. We may not think of it then, but it will be recalled to our minds in after years, when the gloomy grave or a fearful living separation has placed her far beyond our reach, and her sweet voice of sympathy and consolation for the various ills attendant upon us sounds in our ears no more. How deeply then we regret a thousand deeds that we have done contrary to her gentle admonitions! How we sigh for those days once more, that we may retrieve what we have done amiss and make her kind heart glad with happiness! Alas! once gone they can never be recalled, and we grow mournfully sad with the bitter reflection.

"Oh, my mother!" I cried aloud, "my dearly beloved mother! Would I someday behold her again? Should I ever return to my native land? Would I find her among the living? If not, if not, heavens! what a sad, what a painful thought!" and instantly I found my eyes swimming in tears and my frame trembling with nervous agitation. But I would hope for the best. Gradually I did become calm; then I thought of my husband, and what might be his fate. It was sad at best, I well knew. And lastly, though I tried to avoid it, I thought of Mary; sweet, lost, but dearly beloved Mary; I could see her gentle features; I could hear her plaintive voice, soft and silvery as running waters, and sighed a long, deep sigh as I thought of her murdered. Could I never behold her again? No; she was dead, perished by the cruel, relentless savage. Silence brooded over the world; not a sound broke the solemn repose of nature; the summer breeze had rocked itself to rest in the willow boughs, and the broad-faced, familiar moon seemed alive and toiling as it climbed slowly up a cloudless sky, passing starry sentinels, whose nightly challenge was lost in vast vortices of blue as they paced their ceaseless round in the mighty camp of constellations. With my eyes fixed upon my gloomy surroundings of tyranny, occasionally a splash of moonshine silvered the ground. I watched and reflected. Oh, hallowed days of my blessed girlhood! They rise before me now like holy burning stars breaking out in a stormy, howling night, making the blackness blacker still. The short, happy springtime of life, so full of noble aspirations, and glowing hopes of my husband's philanthropic schemes of charitable projects in the future.

We had planned so much for the years to come, when, prosperous and happy, we should be able to distribute some happiness among those whose fate might be mingled with ours, and in the pursuit of our daily avocations we would find joy and peace. But, alas! for human hopes and expectations!

It is thus with our life. We silently glide along, little dreaming about the waves which will so soon sweep over us, dashing us up against the rocks, or stranding us forever. We do not dream that we shall ever wreck, until the greater wave comes over us, and we bend beneath its power.

If some mighty hand could unroll the future to our gaze or set aside the veil which enshrouds it, what pictures would be presented to our trembling hearts? No; let it be as the All-wise hath ordained— a closed-up tomb, only revealed as the events occur, for could we bear them with the fortitude we should if they were known beforehand? Shrinking from it, we would say, "Let the cup pass from me."

XVII

A Prairie on Fire

IN OCTOBER, we were overtaken by a prairie fire. At this season of the year, the different plants and grass, parched by a hot sun, are ready to blaze in a moment if ignited by the tiniest spark, which is often borne along by the wind from some of the many campfires.

With frightful rapidity we saw it extend in all directions, but we were allowed time to escape.

The Indians ran like wild animals before the flames, uttering yells like demons; and great walls of fire from the right and from the left advanced toward us, hissing, crackling, and threatening to unite and swallow us up in their raging fury.

We were amid calcined trees, which fell with a thundering crash, blinding us with clouds of smoke, and were burned by the showers of sparks, which poured upon us from all directions.

The conflagration assumed formidable proportions; the forest shrunk up in the terrible grasp of the flames, and the prairie presented one sheet of fire, in the midst of which the wild animals, driven from their dens and hiding places by this unexpected catastrophe, ran about mad with terror.

The sky gleamed with blood-red reflection, and

the impetuous wind swept both flames and smoke before it.

The Indians were terrified in the extreme on seeing around them the mountain heights lighted up like beacons to show the entire destruction. The earth became hot, while immense troops of buffalo made the ground tremble with their furious tread, and their bellowings of despair would fill with terror the hearts of the bravest men.

Everyone became frightened and started running about the camp as if struck by insanity.

The fire continued to advance majestically, as it were, swallowing up everything in its way. It was preceded by countless animals of various kinds that bounded along with howls of fear, pursued by the fast moving scourge which threatened to overtake them at every step.

A dense smoke, laden with sparks, was already passing over the camp. Ten minutes more and all would be over with us, I thought, when I saw the squaws pressing the children to their bosoms.

The presence of imminent peril had taken all self-possession from the tribesmen. The flames had joined to form an immense circle in which our camp had become the center, but, fortunately, the strong breeze which, up to that moment, had lent wings to the conflagration, suddenly subsided and there was not a breath of air stirring.

The progress of the fire slackened. Providence seemed to grant us time.

The camp presented a strange aspect. On bended knee I prayed fervently. The fire continued to approach with its vanguard of wild beasts.

The Indians, old and young, male and female, began to pull up the grass by the roots all about the camp, then lassoed the horses and hobbled them in the center, and, in a few moments, a large space was cleared, where the herbs and grass had been pulled up with the feverish rapidity which all display in the fear of death.

Some of the Indians went to the extremity of the space where the grass had been pulled up, and formed a pile of grass and plants with their feet; then, with their flint set fire to the mass, and thus caused "fire to fight fire," as they called it. This was done in different directions. A curtain of flames rose rapidly around us, and for some time the camp was almost concealed beneath a vault of fire.

It was a moment of intense and awful anxiety. By degrees the flames became less fierce, the air purer; the smoke dispersed, the roaring diminished, and, at length, we were able to recognize each other in this horrible chaos.

A sigh of relief burst from every heart. Our camp was saved! After the first moments of joy were over, the camp was put in order, and all felt the necessity of repose after the terrible anxieties of the preceding hours; and also to give the ground time enough to cool, so that it might be traveled over by people and horses.

The next day we prepared for departure. Tents were folded and packages were placed upon the ponies, and our caravan was soon pursuing its journey under the direction of the chief, who rode in advance of our band.

The appearance of the prairie was much changed since the previous evening. In various places the burnt earth was a heap of smoking ashes; charred trees, still standing, appeared as ghoulish skeletons. The fire still roared on, but at a great distance, and the horizon was still obscured by smoke.

The horses advanced with caution over the uneven ground, constantly stumbling over the bones of animals that had fallen victims to the flames.

Our traveling course wound along a narrow ravine, the dried bed of a torrent, deeply enclosed between two hills. The ground consisted of round pebbles, which caused the horses to slip and augmented the difficulty of the march, which was rendered more toilsome to me by the rays of the sun falling directly upon my uncovered head and face.

The day passed away thus, and, aside from the fatigue which oppressed me, the day's journey was unbroken by any incident.

At evening, we once again camped upon a barren plain, but in the distance we could see an appearance of verdure, affording great consolation, for we could now enter a spot spared by the conflagration.

At sunrise next morning, we were on the march toward this oasis in the desert.

XVIII

Turned Over to the Blackfeet Sioux

M Y LAST days with the Oglala Sioux were to be marked by a terrible remembrance.

On the first day of October, while the savages lingered in camp about the banks of the Yellowstone River, apparently fearing, yet almost inviting attack by their closeness to the soldiers, a large Mackinaw, or flatboat, was seen coming down the river.

From their hiding places they watched its progress like the tiger waiting for his prey.

At sundown, the unsuspecting travelers pushed their boat toward the shore to camp for the night.

The party consisted of about twenty men, women, and children. Suspecting no danger, they left their arms in the boat.

With a vicious yell, the savages set upon them, dealing death and destruction in rapid strokes.

The defenseless emigrants made an attempt to rush to the boat for arms, but were cut off, and their bleeding bodies dashed into the river as fast as they were slain. Then followed the torture of the women and children.[1]

[1] The editors have been unable to find any contemporary mention of this Sioux massacre of flatboat emigrants on the Yellowstone.

156

Horrible thought! from which all will turn with sickened soul and shuddering cry to Heaven, "How long, O Lord! how long shall such inhuman atrocities go unpunished?"

Not a soul was left alive when that black day's work was complete; and the unconscious river bore away the warm tide of human blood and sinking human forms.

When the warriors returned to our camp, they held high their frightful trophies of bloodstained clothes and ghastly scalps.

My heartsick eyes beheld the dreadful fruits of carnage; and, among the lot, I saw a woman's scalp with heavy chestnut hair, a golden brown, and four feet in length, which had been secured for its beauty. The tempting treasure lost the poor girl her life, which might have been spared; but her glorious locks were needed to hang on the chief's belt.

During that season nearly all the flatboats coming from the mining regions that floated down the Yellowstone River to the Missouri were attacked, and in some instances one or more of the occupants killed. The approach of this boat was known, and the Indians had ample time to plan their attack so that not a soul should escape.

That night the whole camp of braves assembled to celebrate the fearful scalp dance; and from the door of my tent I witnessed the savage spectacle, for I was ill, and, to my great relief, was not forced to join in the horrid ceremony.

A number of squaws occupied the center of the ring they formed, and the pitiless wretches held up the fresh scalps that day reaped from the harvest of death.

Around them circled the frantic braves, flourishing torches and brandishing weapons, and screaming the most ferocious barks and yells, and wild distortions of countenance.

Some repeatedly boasted of bravery and prowess while others lost their own identity in mocking their dying victims in their agony.

Leaping first on one foot, then on the other, accompanying every movement with wild whoops of excitement, they presented a scene which would be never forgotten.

The young brave who bore the beautiful locks as his trophy did not join in the dance. He sat alone, looking sad.

I approached and questioned him, and he replied that he regretted his dead victim. He brought a bloodstained dress from his lodge, and told me it was worn by the girl with the lovely hair, whose eyes haunted him and made him sorry.

After being cognizant of this frightful massacre, I shrank more than ever from my savage companions, and pursued my tasks in hopeless despondence of ever being rescued or restored to civilized life.

One day I was astonished to notice a strange Indian, whom I had never seen before, making signs to me of a mysterious nature.

He indicated by signs that he wanted me to run away with him to the white people, however I had become so suspicious from having been deceived so many times that I turned from him and entered the chief's tent, where, despite his cruelty and harshness to me, I felt comparatively safe.

I afterward saw this Indian, or rather white man or half-breed, as I believe him to have been, though he could not, nor would not, speak a word of English. His long hair hung loosely about his shoulders, and was of a dark brown color. He had in no respect the appearance of an Indian, but rather that of a wild, reckless frontier desperado. I had never seen him before, though he seemed well-known in the camp.

One thing that perhaps made me more suspicious and afraid to trust anyone was a knowledge of the fact that many of the Indians, who had lost relatives in the recent battles with General Sully, were thirsting for my blood, and would have been pleased to decoy me far enough away to vent their vengeance, yet be safe from the expected fury of the old chief, my taskmaster.

One day this stranger came into a tent where I was and showed me a small pocket Bible that had belonged to my husband, and was presented to him by his now sainted mother many years before. His object was to assure me that I might trust him, but such an instinctive mistrust of the man had taken possession of me that I refused to believe him. At last, he became enraged and threatened to kill me if I would not go with him.

I plead with him to give me the Bible, but he refused. How dear it would have been to me from association, and what strength and comfort I would have received from its precious promises, shut out as I was from my world and all religious privileges.

Soon after the foregoing incident, the old chief and his three sisters went away on a journey, and I was sent to live with some of his relatives, accompanied by my little companion, Yellow Bird. We traveled all day to reach our destination, a small Indian village. The family I was to live with until the return of the chief and his sisters consisted of a very old Indian, his squaw, and a young girl.

I had a dread of going among strangers, but was thankful for the kindness with which I was received by this old couple. I was very tired, and so sad and depressed that I cared not to ask for anything. The old squaw, seeming to understand my feelings, considerately placed before me meat and water, and kindly ministered to my wants in every way their means would allow.

I was with this family nearly three weeks and was treated with almost affectionate kindness, not only by them but by every member of the little community. The children would come to see me and manifest in various ways their interest in me. They would say, "Wasechawea (white woman) looks sad; I want to shake hands with her."

I soon started to adapt myself to my new surroundings and became more happy and contented than I had ever yet been since my captivity began. My time was occupied in assisting the motherly old squaw in her sewing and other domestic work.

On one occasion a dark cloud came between us. The old chief had given orders that I was not to be permitted to go out among the other villagers alone, orders which were not told to me. Feeling a new sense of freedom, I had sometimes gone out, and on one occasion, having been invited into different tipis by the squaws, staid so long that the old Indian sent for me and seemed angry when I returned. He said it was good for me to stay in his tent, but bad to go out among the others. I pacified him by saying I knew his home was pleasant and I was happy there, and that I did not know it was bad to go among the other tents.

The old chief returned, finally, and my brief season of enjoyment ended. He seemed to delight in torturing me, often pinching my arms until they were black and blue. Regarding me as the cause of his wounded arm, he was determined that I should suffer with him.

While in this camp, "Man-Afraid-of-His-Horses" arrived, and I was made aware of his high standing as a chief and warrior by the feasting and dancing which followed. He was splendidly mounted and equipped, as also was another Indian who accompanied him.

I have since learned from my husband that the treacherous chief made such statements of his influence with the hostile Indians as to induce my husband to purchase an expensive outfit for him in the hope of my release. I conversed with him several times, and though he told me that he was from the Platte, he said nothing of the real errand on which he was sent, but returned to the fort and reported to Mr. Kelly that the band had moved and I could not be found.

Captain Fisk had made known to General Sully the fact of my being among the Indians, and the efforts he had made for my release. Then when the Blackfeet presented themselves before the General, asking for peace and avowing their weariness of hostility, however anxious to purchase arms, ammunition, and necessaries for the approaching winter, he replied:

"I want no peace with you. You hold in captivity a white woman. Deliver her up to us and we will believe in your professions. But unless you do, we will bring soldiers as numerous as the trees on the Missouri River and exterminate the Indians."

The Blackfeet assured General Sully that they held no white woman in their possession, but that I was among the Oglalas.

"As you are friendly with them," said the General, "go to them and secure her, and we will then reward you for so doing."

The Blackfeet warriors appeared openly in the

village a few days afterward, and declared their intentions, stating in council the determination of General Sully.

The Oglalas were not afraid, they said, and refused to let me go. They held solemn council for two days, and at last resolved that the Blackfeet should take me as a ruse so as to enable them to enter the fort, and a wholesale slaughter should exterminate the soldiers.

While thus deliberating as to what they thought best—part of them willing, the other half refusing to let me go—Hunkiapa, a warrior, came into the lodge and ordered me out.

He led me into a lodge where there were fifty warriors, painted and armed—their bows strung and their quivers full of arrows.

From thence, the whole party, including three squaws, who, noting my extreme fear, accompanied me as we started toward a creek, where we were to find five horses and warriors to accompany us to the Blackfeet village.

After placing me on a horse, we were rapidly pursuing our way when a party of the Oglalas, who were unwilling to let me go caught up to us with the purpose of reclaiming me.

Both groups parleyed for a time, and, finally, after a solemn promise on the part of my new captors that I should be returned safely, and that I should be cared for and kindly treated, we were allowed to proceed.

During their parleying, one of the warriors ordered me to alight from the horse, pointing a pistol to my breast. Many of them clamored for my life, but, finally, they settled the matter, and permitted us to proceed on our journey.

After so many prior escapes from death, this last seemed miraculous; but God willed it otherwise, and to Him I owe my grateful homage.

It was a bitter trial for me to be obliged to go with this new and stranger tribe. I was unwilling to exchange my life for an unknown one, and especially as my companionship with the sisters of the chief had been such as to protect me from injury or insult. A sort of security and safety was felt in the lodge of the chief, which now the fear of my new position made me appreciate still more.

Savages they were, and I had longed to be free from them; but now I parted with them with regret and misgiving.

Though my new masters, for such I considered them, held out promise of liberty and restoration to my friends, knowing the treacherous nature of the Indians, I doubted them. Surely, the Oglalas had treated me at times with great harshness and cruelty, yet I had never suffered from any of them the slightest personal or unchaste insult. Let me bear testimony to this redeeming feature in their treatment of me.

At the time of my capture, I became the exclusive property of Ottawa, the head chief, a man more than seventy-five years old and partially blind, yet whose power over the band was absolute. After receiving a severe wound in a melee I have already given an account of, I was compelled to become his nurse or medicine woman; and my services as such were so appreciated, that harsh and cruel as he might be, it was dangerous for others to offer me insult or injury; and to this fact, doubtlessly, I owe my escape from a fate worse than death.

The Blackfeet are a band of the Sioux nation; consequently are allies in battle. The chief dared not refuse on this account; besides he was wounded badly and was an invalid.

The Blackfeet left three of their best horses as a guarantee for my safe return.

The chief of the Oglalas had expressed the wish that, if the Great Spirit should summon him away, that I might be killed in order to become his attendant to the spirit land.

It was now the commencement of November, and their way seemed to lead to the snowy regions, where the cold might prove unendurable.

When I heard the pledge given by the Blackfeet, my fears abated; and hope sprang buoyant at the thought of again being within the reach of my own people. Now, I felt confident that once in the fort I could frustrate their plans by warning the officers of their intentions thereby thwarting their savage treachery and punishing the instigators.

XIX

Indian Customs

D<small>URING</small> my enforced sojourn with the Oglalas, I had abundant opportunity to observe the manners and customs peculiar to a race of people living so near, and yet of whom so little is known.

Nothing can be more simple in its arrangement than an Indian camp when journeying, and especially when on the warpath. The camping ground, when practicable, is adjacent to a stream of water and near timber. After reaching the spot selected, the ponies are unloaded by the squaws and turned loose to graze. The tents, or "tipis," are put up, and wood and water brought for cooking purposes. All drudgery of this kind is performed by the squaws since an Indian brave scorns as degrading all kinds of labor not incident to the chase or the warpath.

An Indian tipi is composed of several dressed skins, usually of the buffalo, sewed together and stretched over a number of poles, the larger ones containing as many as twenty of these poles, which are fifteen to twenty feet long. They are of yellow pine, stripped of bark, and are used as "travois" while traveling. Three poles are lashed together near the top and then raised into an upright position, the bottoms are then spread out as far as the

166

fastening at the top will permit. Other poles are laid into the crotch formed at the top, and spread out in a circular line with the three first put up. This comprises the frame work and is ready to receive the covering, which is raised to the top by means of a rawhide rope, after which a squaw seizes each lower corner, which are then fastened together with wooden pins. To assist, a squaw gets down on all fours, forming a perch upon which the tallest squaw of the family mounts and inserts the pins as high as she can reach. A square opening in the tent serves for a door, and is entered in a stooping posture. A piece of hide hangs loosely over this opening, and is kept in position by a heavy piece of wood fastened at the bottom.

When in position, the Indian tipi is of the same shape as the Sibley tent. In the middle is built a fire where all the cooking is done; a hole at the top affording egress for the smoke. The preparation for a meal is a very simple affair. Meat was almost their only article of diet, and was generally roasted or rather warmed through over the fire, though sometimes it was partially boiled, and always eaten without salt or bread. They have no particular time for eating; will fast all of one day and perhaps eat a dozen times the next.

The outer edge of the tent contains the beds of the family, which are composed of buffalo robes and blankets. These are snugly rolled up during the day, and do service as seats.

If there is reason to suppose an enemy is near, fire is not allowed in camp; and in that case each one satisfies appetite as best he or she can, but generally with "pa-pa," or dried buffalo meat.

An Indian camp at close of day presents a most animated picture: squaws passing to and fro, loaded with wood and water, or meat, or guiding the sledges drawn by dogs; groups of dusky warriors squatting on the ground around fires built in the open air, smoking their pipes or repairing weapons while recounting their exploits; half dressed and naked children capering about in childish glee, all together furnishing a picture of the nomadic life of these Indians. Not more than ten minutes are required to set up an Indian village.

When it becomes necessary to move a village, a fact that is never known to the people, a crier goes through the camp, shouting, "Egalakapo! Egalakapo!" When heard, all the squaws drop whatever work they may be engaged in, and in an instant are busy as bees, taking down tipis, bringing in the ponies and dogs, and loading them; and in less than fifteen minutes the cavalcade is on the march.

The squaws accompany the men when they go to hunt buffalo, and as fast as the animals are killed, they strip off their hides, and then cut off the meat in strips about three feet long, three to four inches wide, and two inches thick; and such is their skill that the bones will be left intact and as free from meat as though they had been boiled. The meat

Indian Camp Scene
Courtesy Denver Public Library

is then brought into the camp and hung up to dry.

The medicine men treat all diseases nearly alike. The principal efforts are directed to expelling the spirit, whatever it may be, which it is expected the medicine man will soon discover, and having informed the friends what it is, he usually requires them to be in readiness to shoot it, as soon as he shall succeed in expelling it.

Incantations and ceremonies are used, intended to secure the aid of the spirit, or spirits, the Indian worships. When he thinks he has succeeded, the medicine man gives the command, and from two to six or more guns are fired at the door of the tent to destroy the spirit as it passes out.

Many of these medicine men depend wholly on conjuring, sitting by the bedside of the patient, making gestures and frightful noises, shaking rattles, and endeavoring, by all means in their power, to frighten away the evil spirit. They regularly use fumigation and are very fond of aromatic substances, using and burning cedar along with many different plants to thoroughly cleanse the tent in which the sick person lies.

The native plants, roots, herbs, and so forth, are used freely, and are efficacious.

They are very careful to conceal from each other, except for an initiated few, as well as from white men, a knowledge of the plants used as medicine, probably believing that their efficacy, in some measure, depends on this concealment.

There is a tall, branching plant, growing abundantly in the open woods and prairies near the Missouri River, which is used chiefly by the Indians as a purgative, and is *euphorbia corrallata*, well known to the botanist.

Medicines are generally kept in bags made of the skin of some animal.

All the drinks which are given the sick to quench thirst are astringent, sometimes bitter and sometimes slightly mucilaginous.

The most common is called red-root (*ceanothus canadensis*), a plant abounding in the western prairies, although they seem to have more faith in some ceremony.[1]

A dance peculiar to the tribe where I was, called the pipe dance, is worth mentioning and is called by the Indians a good medicine. A small fire is kindled in the village, and around this the dancers, which usually consist of young men, collect, each one seated upon a robe.

The presiding genius is a chief or a medicine man, who seats himself by a fire. He holds a long pipe which he prepares for smoking. Offering it first to the Great Spirit, he then extends it toward the north, south, east, and west; muttering unintelligibly. Meanwhile an equally august personage beats a

[1]This was probably a western variety of *ceanothus Americanus*, commonly called New Jersey tea and used by eastern Indians as a wash for syphilitic sores and for eye diseases or to help in blood coagulation.

drum while singing, leaping, and smoking. The master of ceremonies sits calmly looking on, puffing away with all the vigor imaginable.

The dance closes with piercing yells and barking like frightened dogs. It lasts an hour or more.

When the mother gives birth to her child, it is not uncommon for no other person to be present. She then lives in a hut or lodge by herself until the child is twenty-five to thirty days old. She then takes it to its father, who sees his child for the first time. It is an uncommon occurrence that an Indian woman loses her life in parturition.

When the child is old enough to run alone, it is relieved of its swathings, and if the weather is not too cold, it is sent off without a particle of clothing to protect it or impede the action of its limbs. In this manner it is allowed to remain until it is several years old, when it receives a limited wardrobe.

Despite the rugged and exposed life they lead, there are comparatively few cripples and deformed persons among them. It is said that deformed infants are regarded as unprofitable and a curse from the Great Spirit. They are disposed of by death soon after birth. Sometimes, at the death of a mother, the infant is also interred. An incident of this kind was related to me. A whole family had been carried off by smallpox except an infant. Those who were not sick had as much to do as they could conveniently attend to, consequently there was no one willing to take charge of the little orphan. It was placed in the arms of its dead mother, enveloped in blankets and a buffalo robe, and then laid on a scaffold in the tribe's burying place. Its cries were heard for some time, but at last grew fainter, and finally were hushed altogether in the cold embrace of death with the moaning wind sounding its requiem and the wolves howling in the surrounding gloom, a fitting dirge for so sad a fate.

The Indians believe that God or the Great Spirit created the universe and all things just as they exist.

They believe the sun to be a large body of heat, and that it revolves around the earth. Some believe it is a ball of fire. They do not comprehend the revolution of the earth around the sun. They suppose the sun literally rises and sets, and that our present theory is an invention of the white man, and that he is not sincere when he says the earth moves around the sun.

They think that paradise or the happy hunting grounds is above, but where, they have no definite idea, though believing the future a happier state. They regard skill in hunting or success in war as the passport to eternal happiness and plenty, where there is no cold or wet season. Still they all acknowledge, it is the gift of the Wa-hon Tonka, the Great Spirit.

The manner of disposing of their dead is one of the peculiar customs of the Indians of the plains which impresses the beholder for the first time most forcibly. Four forked posts are set up and on them a platform is laid, high enough to be out of reach of wolves or other carniverous animals, and upon this the body is placed, wrapped in blankets or buffalo robes, and sometimes both, according to the circumstances of the deceased, and these are wound securely with a strip of buffalo hide. If in the vicinity of timber, the body is placed on a platform, securely fixed in the crotch of a high tree. The wrappings of buffalo robe or blankets protect the body from ravenous birds that hover around, attracted by the scent of an anticipated feast.

All that pertained to the dead while living, in the way of furs, blankets, weapons, cooking utensils, etc., are also deposited with the body. On occasion the horse which belonged to the deceased was shot. They believe that the spirit wanders off to distant hunting grounds, and because it might pass over a country where there is no game, a quantity of dried buffalo meat is usually left with the body for its subsistence. While on a journey, these burial places are held sacred like those of a Christian nation, and if a tribe is passing such localities they will make a detour rather than go the more direct road by the resting place of their dead, while the relatives leave the trail and go alone to the spot and there renew and repeat their mourning as on the occasion of his death. They also leave presents for the dead of such little trinkets as he most prized before he departed to his new hunting grounds.

The boys are early taught the arts of war. A bow

Sioux Indian Above-Ground Burial

Courtesy American Heritage Center,
University of Wyoming

and arrows are among the first presents an Indian youth receives from his parents, and he is soon instructed in their use. Indeed, the skill of a hunter seems to be a natural endowment, and although some are more accurate and active than others, they all shoot with wonderful precision and surprising aptitude, seeming to inherit a passionate love for the sport of the chase.

The Indian boy receives no name until some distinguishing trait of character or feat suggests one, and it may vary from time to time as more fitting ones are suggested. Some of the names are very odd, and some quite vulgar.

The wife is sometimes wooed and won, as if there was something of sentiment in the Indian character, but more often is purchased without the wooing. When the desired object is particularly attractive and of a good family, both the courting and purchasing may be required. When a young brave goes courting, he decorates himself in his best attire, instinctively divining that appearances weigh much in the eyes of a forest belle or dusky maiden, who receives him bashfully, for a certain kind of modesty is inherent in Indian girls, which is rather incongruous when considered in relation to their peculiar mode of life. Discretion and propriety are most carefully observed, and the lovers are seated side-by-side in silence. At times he produces presents for her acceptance. These express a variety of sentiment and refer to distinct and separate things; some signifying love; some, strength; some, bravery. Others allude to the life of servitude she is expected to live if she becomes his wife. If they are accepted graciously and the maiden remains seated, it is thought to be equivalent to an assurance of love on her part and is acted upon accordingly. Although no woman's life is made less slavish by the marriage connection, and no one is treated with respect, it is scarcely known in Indian life that a girl has remained unmarried even to middle age.

When a chief desires to multiply the number of his wives, he often marries several sisters, if they can be had, not because of any particular fancy he may have for any but the one who first captivated him, but because he thinks there will be more harmony in the household when they are of one family. Not even squaws can live happily together when each has a part interest in the same man as their husband. Polygamy is generally considered inconsistent with the female character, whether in barbarism or civilization.[2]

As many skins as they can transport on their ponies, of the game killed while on their hunts, are dressed by the squaws and then taken to some trading post, military station, or agency, and bartered off for such articles as are most desired by them, such as beads, paints, etc., and powder, lead, and

[2]Strictly speaking, the Indians (and the Mormons) practiced polygyny, having more than one wife at the same time. Polygamy allowed for multiple wives or husbands.

caps. They are willing to allow much more proportionately for ammunition than any other articles. They are most outrageously swindled by the traders whom our Government licenses to trade with them. A buffalo robe which the trader sells for from ten to fifteen dollars is bought from the Indians for a pint cup of sugar and a small handful of bullets, while furs of all kinds are exchanged for paints and trinkets at equally disproportionate rates. The Indians know they are being cheated whenever they barter with the white traders, but they have no remedy as there is no competition, and this causes much of their disaffection.

Buffalo robes, bearskins, and deer and antelope skins are brought in in great numbers. Beaver and otter are hunted expressly for their furs.

The Indians are almost universally fond of whisky and have a strong propensity for gambling. They will risk at cards almost everything they own, and if unsuccessful, appear quite resigned to their loss, continually resting in the gambler's hope of "better luck next time."

The squaws play a game with small bones of oblong shape, which seems to have a great fascination for them, as I have known them to spend whole days and nights at it, and in many instances gambling away everything they owned. Five of these pieces are used, each possessing a relative value in the game, designated by spots from one to five on one side, the other being blank. They are placed in a dish or small basket, which is shaken and then hit upon the ground with a jar, tossing the pieces over, and according to the number of spots up, so is the game decided, very similar, I imagine, to the white man's game of "high-die."

They have a peculiar way of defining time. When they wish to designate an hour of the day, they point to the position the sun should be in at that time. The number of days is the number of sleeps. Their next division of time is the number of moons instead of our months; and the seasons are indicated by the state of vegetation. For instance, spring is when the grass begins to grow and the autumn is when the leaves fall from the trees, while years are indicated by the season of snows.

There is a language of signs common to all the tribes by which one tribe may communicate with another without being able to speak or understand its dialect. This allows each tribe to be known by some particular sign.

The Indian is noted for his power of endurance for both fatigue and physical pain. I have thought much about the fear patented by these reputedly brave barbarians; they seem to be borne down with a most tormenting fear for their personal safety at all times whether at home or roaming for plunder or when hunting, and yet courage is made a virtue among them while cowardice is the unpardonable sin. When compelled to meet death, they seem to assemble sullen, obstinate defiance of their doom, which makes the most of a dreaded necessity rather than seek a preparation to meet it with submission, which they often dissemble but never possess.

Instinct, more than reason, is the guide of the red man. He repudiates improvement and despises manual effort. For ages his heart has been embedded in moral pollution.

The blanket, as worn by the Indian, is an insuperable barrier to his advance in arts or agriculture. When this is forever dispensed with, then his hands will be free to grasp the mechanic's tools or guide the plow. It is both graceful and chaste in their eyes, and to adopt the white man's dress is a great obstacle, a requirement too humiliating, for they have personal as well as national pride. No hat is worn, but the head is covered with feathers and rude ornaments. A heavy mass of wampum, at times extremely expensive, adorns the neck. Often, the entire rim of each ear is pierced with holes and adorned with jewels of silver or something resembling it.

The Indian does everything through motives of policy. He has none of the kindlier feelings of humanity in him. He is as devoid of gratitude as he is hypocritical and treacherous. He observes a treaty or promise only so long as it is dangerous for him to disregard it, or for his interest, in other ways, to keep it. Cruelty appears to be inherent within them, and is early manifested by the young, who torture birds, turtles, or any other small animal that may fall into their hands. They delight in it, while the pleasure of the adult from torturing his prisoners is unquestionable. They are inveterate beggars, but never give, unless with a view to receive a more valuable present in return.

The white man, he has been taught, is his enemy, and he has become the most implacable enemy of the white man. His most fiendish murders of the innocent is his sweetest revenge for a wrong that has been done by another.

The youth are very fond of war. They have no other ambition and pant for the glory of battle, longing for the notes of the war song, that they may rush in and win the feathers of a brave. They listen to the stories of the old men as they recall the stirring scenes of their youth, or sing their war songs, which form only a boasting recapitulation of their daring and bravery. They yearn for the glory of war which is the only path to distinction. Having no arts or industrial pursuits, the tribes are fast waning from war, exposure, and disease.

Only a few of the tribes cultivate the soil because the nature of the Indian degrades all labor not incident to the chase or the warpath. Notwithstanding the efforts of missionaries, and the vast sums of money expended by the Government to place them on reservations and teach them the art of agriculture, the attempts to civilize the Indian in such a way may be considered almost a complete failure. The results bear no comparison to their cost.

Their ideas of the extent and power of the white

race are very limited, and after I had learned the language sufficiently to converse with them, I frequently tried to explain to them the superior advantages of the white man's mode of living. They would ask me many questions as to the number of the white men on this side of the big water and how far that extended; and on being told of two big oceans, they would ask if the whites owned the big country on the other side and if there were any Indians there. Many of my statements were received with incredulity and I was often called a liar, especially when I told of the number and rapid increase of the white race. Sometimes the older ones would get angry. The younger ones were often eager listeners, and especially in times of scarcity and hunger would they gather around me to learn about the white man, and then would I endeavor to impress them with the advantages of a fixed home and tilling the soil over their wild, roaming life.

XX

Getting Along in My New Camp

THE Blackfeet village was one hundred and fifty miles from the Oglalas, and the way thither lay often over the tops of bare and sandy hills.[1]

On the summits of these heights I found shells such as are picked up at the seaside. The Indians accounted for their appearance there by saying that once a great sea rolled over the face of the country and only one man in a boat escaped with his family. He had sailed about in the boat until the waters retired to their place, and, living there, became the father of all the Indians.

These savages proved very kind to me. Though the Blackfeet are regarded by the whites as quite vindictive and hostile, they showed me nothing but civility and respect.

On the third morning we reached a small village where we stopped. The Indians of the village were rejoiced to see me, and I recognized many familiar faces among them. They talked to us about their

[1]Based on Indian oral history, Doane Robinson in 1908 located the Blackfeet village as being on Grand River at a point known as Laughing Wood, eight miles above the mouth of Rock Creek (near the present town of Bullhead, South Dakota) which would be about where Rock Creek is crossed by U.S. Highway 12.

mistrust and apprehension lest I had been stolen from the Oglalas; but the Blackfeet assured them to the contrary; and, after further questioning me, they became satisfied and gave us food. Further, they promised to send warriors to our village and to give us another horse.

The journey to the village of the Blackfeet was exceedingly wearisome—completely exhausting me by its length. Additionally, I suffered from the intense cold weather.

Approaching their village, they entered it with loud demonstrations of joy, singing and whooping after the manner of their race, with noises defying description.

I was received with great joy; and even marks of distinction were shown me. That night there was a feast, and everything denoted a time of rejoicing.

My life was now changed—instead of my waiting upon others, they waited upon me.

The day of my arrival in the Blackfeet village was a sad one, indeed, being the first anniversary of my wedding. The songs and shouts of exultation of the Indians seemed like a bitter mockery of my misery and helplessness.

In the village I met many warriors whom I had seen during the summer and knew that they had fought in battles against General Sully. They saw that something had made me sad and asked what it was. I told them it was my birthday.

Soon after my arrival, Egosegalonicha was sent to

me and inquired how I was treated. She particularly wished to know if they were respectful to me, and inquired as to my safety and well-being, and that any remissness on the part of the Blackfeet would be visited with vengeance.

She told me that her people mourned the captive's absence and grieved for her presence. From others I learned the same.

Next morning there was great commotion in the camp which was caused by the arrival of a delegation from the Yanktons. They brought a handsome horse and saddle as a present for me.

The saddle was of exquisite workmanship, being embroidered with beads, and richly decorated with fringe.

The Yanktons desired to purchase me, offering five of their finest horses for me, which made the Blackfeet quite indignant. Because they believed they also had fine horses, they deemed it an insult and returned the horse and its saddle. Fearing my disappointment, they, in council that night, decided to present me with something as worthy as the Yanktons had sent.

Accordingly, at the door of the tent next morning were four of their best animals; eight beautiful robes were brought in by the young men and also given to me.

The Yanktons were told to return to their tribe and if such a message was again sent, the hatchet would be painted and given to them.

This closed the negotiation, but not their efforts to obtain me.

The large reward which had been offered for my recovery caused the Indians much trouble, as frequently large parties from other tribes would come in, offering to purchase me from those who held me captive. Several such instances occurred while I was with the Oglalas; and the Blackfeet were not exempt from similar annoyances.

One day, while in Tall Soldier's tipi, a large body of mounted warriors was seen approaching the village. The women gathered around me and told me I must stay in the tent, concealed. There was much excitement, and all the women seemed frightened. Soon I knew that preparations were being made for a feast on a large scale. The strange warriors came into camp and held a council, at which Tall Soldier made a speech, which, from the distance, I could not understand; they then had a feast and departed. The Blackfeet gave me to understand that the visit of these Indians was on my account as had been that of the Yanktons.

Soon after, I noticed that parties of warriors would leave the camp daily and return, bringing ammunition and goods of various kinds. I learned from the squaws and children that a party of traders from the Platte River had arrived in the neighborhood with four wagons to trade with the Indians, and that they wanted to buy me, but the red men would not part with me. I pretended to the Indians that I did not desire to leave them, but pleaded that I might go with them to see the white men, which was refused, as was also a request that I might write a letter to them.

A few days later all but one of the traders were murdered. The escaped man reached Fort Laramie nearly dead from hunger and exposure, having traveled the hundreds of miles from the Missouri River on foot.

I have since learned that the men were sent out by Mr. Beauvais, a trader near Fort Laramie, with instructions to procure my release if it required all they possessed.[2]

Since learning these facts, I am more than ever convinced that the reluctance of the Indians to give me up grew out of their hope of capturing Fort Sully through my involuntary agency, and securing a greater booty than any ransom offered; and also as a form of revenge for the losses inflicted upon their nation by the soldiers under General Sully.

The Blackfeet appeared in every respect superior to the tribe I had left. The chief, Tall Soldier, displayed at all times the manners and bearing of a natural gentleman.

[2]In February, 1864, Geminien P. Beauvais, a veteran trader born in St. Louis, ran a "ranch"—a trading store—four miles from Fort Laramie and another at the Old California Crossing on the South Platte. Married to a Sioux, he enjoyed a thriving business with both emigrants and Indians until the violence of 1864–65 forced him to sell and retreat to St. Louis.

They kept up an air of friendliness and communicated frequently with the whites; but, in reality, were ready to join any hostile expedition against them, and were with the Oglalas when our train was attacked at the Little Box Elder.

The Blackfeet seemed to be stationary in their village, only sallying out in small parties for plunder and horses; and, during that time, keeping up a succession of entertainments at the tipi of the chief, where a steady arrival of warriors and many Indians from other tribes, who were warmly welcomed, added to the excitement of the days.

I sympathized with the poor wife of the chief, who was the only woman, besides myself, in the tent, and to whose labor all the feasts were due.

She was obliged to dress the meat, make fires, carry water, and wait upon strangers, besides setting the lodge in order.

These unceasing toils she performed alone—the commands of the chief forbidding me to aid her.

While with the Oglalas, not once had I crossed their will or offered resistance to my tasks, however heavy, having learned that obedience and cheerfulness were greatly prized; and it was my conciliating policy that had made them bewail my loss so deeply.

The squaws are very rebellious, often displaying ungovernable and violent temper. They consider their life a servitude, and being beaten at times like animals, and receiving no sort of sympathy, it acts upon them accordingly.

The contrast between them and my patient submission had its effect upon the Indian men, and caused them to miss me when separated from them.

During my sojourn in this village I was invited to every feast and to the various lodges. One day, while I was visiting one of these lodges, a package of letters was given me to read. They had been taken from Captain Fisk's train, and were touchingly beautiful. Some of them were the correspondence of a Mr. Nichols with a young lady to whom he seemed quite tenderly attached. I was called upon to read these letters and explain their meaning to the Indians.

I was removed at different times to various lodges as a sort of concealment; after I learned that the Yanktons had not yet given up the idea of securing me. One night I awoke from my slumbers to behold an Indian bending over me, cutting through the robes which covered me. Fearing to move, I reached out my hand to the squaw who slept near me (whose name was Chahompa Sca—White Sugar), pinching her to arouse her, which had its effect; for she immediately arose and gave the alarm, after which the Indian fled. This caused great excitement in the camp and many threats were made against the Yanktons.

The intense cold and furious storms that followed my arrival among the Blackfeet precluded the possibility of their setting out immediately on the proposed journey to Fort Sully.

The snowdrifts had rendered the mountain passes impassable, and the chief informed me that they must wait until they were free from danger before taking leave of the shelter and security of their protected village.

XXI

"Am I Free, Indeed Free?"

JUMPING BEAR, who rescued me from the revengeful arrow of the Indian whose horse the chief shot, one day presented himself to me and reminded me of my indebtedness to him for saving my life.

Trembling with fear, I listened to his avowal of more than ordinary feelings, during which he assured me that I had no cause to fear him—that he had always liked white women, and would be more than a friend to me.

I replied that I did not fear him; that I felt grateful to him for his kindness and protection, but that unless he proved his friendship for me, no persuasion could induce me to listen.

"Will you carry a letter to my people at the fort, delivering it into the hands of the great chief there? They will amply reward you for your effort on behalf of their sister; they will give you many presents and you will return rich."

"I dare not go," he answered. "Nor could I get back before the warriors came to our village."

"My people will give you a fast horse," said I, "and you may return speedily. Go now and prove your friendship by taking the letter and returning with your prizes."

I assured him that the letter contained nothing that would harm him or his people; that I had written about him and his kindness, and of his goodwill toward them. After many lengthy interviews, during which the women of the lodge had used their influence, I, at last, prevailed upon him to go. After invoking the bright moon as a witness to his pledge of honor and truth, he started on his journey, bearing the letter which I believed was to seal my fate for weal or woe. In the moonlight I watched his retreating form, imploring Heaven to grant the safe delivery of the little message upon which so much depended.

Daring and venturesome deed! Should he prove false to me and allow anyone outside the fort to see the letter, my doom was inevitable.

Many days of intense anxiety were passed after his departure. The squaws, fearing that I had made a fearful mistake in sending him, were continually asking questions, and it was with a large degree of difficulty that I could allay their anxiety and stop them from disclosing the secret to the other women in the village.

The contents of the letter were a warning to the "Big Chief" and the soldiers of an intended attack on the fort and the massacre of the garrison, using me as a ruse to enable them to get inside the fort. It was also a desperate plea for them to rescue me, if possible.

The messenger reached the fort and was received

by the officer of the day, Lieutenant Hesselberger,[1] and conducted to the commander of the post, Major House,[2] and Adjutant Pell,[3] who had been left there to treat with the Indians on my account.

General Sully had gone to Washington, but every necessary precaution was taken to secure the fort.

Jumping Bear received a suit of clothes and some presents, and was sent back with a letter for me, but I never saw him again. These facts I learned after my arrival at Fort Sully.

The night before departing from the Blackfeet village en route to the fort, I was lying awake and heard the chief address his men seriously upon the subject of their wrongs at the hands of the whites. I now understood and spoke the Indian tongue readily, and so comprehended his speech, which, as near as I can recollect, was as follows:

"Friends and sons, listen to my words. You are a

[1]Germany-born First Lieutenant Gustav A. Hesselberger joined the Sixth Iowa Cavalry early in 1863 and served until 1871. A strong supporter of Fanny Kelly, he was also instrumental in negotiating the release of Mary Box and her three daughters from the Kiowas in 1866.

[2]Major Albert E. House of the Sixth Iowa Cavalry was a native of Delhi, Iowa, where he entered law practice after his army experience.

[3]Captain John H. Pell, a New Yorker, enlisted in the First Minnesota Infantry in 1861 and eventually became assistant adjutant general of the regiment. Before he was mustered out in 1865, he had fought at South Mountain, both battles of Bull Run, and half a dozen other encounters in the South. He was also with General Sully's 1864 campaign against the Sioux.

great and powerful band of our people. The inferior race, who have encroached upon our rights and territories, justly deserve hatred and destruction. These intruders came among us and we took them by the hand. We believed them to be friends and true speakers; they have shown us how false and cruel they can be.

"They build forts to live in and shoot from with their big guns. Our people fall before them. Our game is chased from the hills. Our women are taken from us and made to forsake our lodges. They have been wronged and deceived.

"It has only been four or five moons since they drove us to desperation, killed our brothers, and burned our tipis. The Indian cries for vengeance! There is no truth nor friendship in the white man; deceit and bitterness are in his words.

"Meet them with equal cunning. Show them no mercy. They are but few, we are many. Whet your knives and string your bows; sharpen the tomahawk and load the rifle.

"Let the wretches die, who have stolen our lands, and we will be free to roam over the soil that was our fathers'. We will come home bravely from battle. Our songs shall rise among the hills, and every tipi shall be hung with the scalp locks of our foes."

This declaration of hostilities was received with grunts of approval; and silently the war preparations went on, so that I might not know the evil design hidden beneath the mask of friendship.

That night, as if in preparation for the work he had planned, the gracious chief beat his poor, tired squaw unmercifully because she murmured at her never-ending labor and heavy tasks.

His deportment to me was as courteous as though he had been educated in civilized life; indeed, had he not betrayed so much ignorance of the extent and power of the American nation in his address to his band, I should have thought him an educated Indian, who had traveled among the whites. Yet in his brutal treatment of his squaw, his savage nature asserted itself and reminded me that, although better served than formerly, I was still among savages.

Morning finally came to my sleepless night and I arose, still worried lest some terrible intervention should come between me and the longed-for journey to the abodes of white men.

The day before leaving the Blackfeet village, I gave all my Indian trinkets to a little girl who had been my constant companion, and because of her gentle and affectionate interest in the captive white woman, she had created within me a feeling akin to love. She was half-white and was granddaughter of a chief called Wichunkiapa, who also treated me with kindness.

The morning after the chief's address to his warriors, the savages were all ready for the road, and, mounting in haste, sent up their farewell chant as they wound in a long column out of the village.

I have frequently been asked, since my release

back to civilization, how I dressed while with the Indians, and whether I was clothed as the squaws were. A description of my appearance as I rode out of the Indian village that morning will satisfy curiosity on this point.

My dress was made up of a narrow, white cotton gown, composed of only two breadths, reaching below the knee and fastened at the waist with a red scarf; moccasins, embroidered with beads and porcupine quills, covered my feet, and a robe over my shoulders completed my wardrobe.

While with the Oglalas, I wore around my arms great brass rings that had been forced on me, some of them fitting so tight that they lacerated my arms severely, leaving scars that I shall ever retain as mementos of my experience in Indian ornamentation. I was also painted as the squaws were, but never voluntarily applied the article.

It was winter and the ground was covered with snow, but so cold was the air that its surface bore the horses' feet on its hard, glittering breast, only breaking through occasionally in the deep gullies.

It was two hundred miles from the Blackfeet village to Fort Sully, in the middle of winter, and the weather intensely cold, the effects from which my ill-clad body suffered severely. I was forced to walk a great part of the way to keep from freezing. Hoping for deliverance, yet dreading the treacherous plans of the Indians for the capture of the fort and massacre of its garrison might prove successful and my return to captivity inevitable, I struggled on, striving to bear with patience the mental and bodily ills from which I suffered. My great fear was that my letter had not fallen into the right hands.

On our journey we came in sight of a few lodges, and in among the timber we camped for the night. While visiting in one of the lodges, to my surprise, a gentlemanly figure came upon me dressed in latest style. It astonished me to meet this gentlemanly-looking, well-mannered person under such peculiar circumstances. He drew quite near, then addressed me courteously.

"This is cold weather for traveling. Do you not find it so?" he inquired.

"Not when I find myself going in the right direction," I replied.

I asked him if he lived in that vicinity, supposing, of course, from the presence of a white man in our camp, that we must be near some fort, trading post, or white settlement.

He smiled and said, "I am a dweller in the hills and confess that civilized life has no charms for me. I find in freedom and nature all the elements requisite for happiness."

Having been separated from the knowledge and interests of national affairs just when the struggle agitating our country was at its height, I asked the question:

"Has Richmond been taken?"

"No, nor never will be," was the reply.

Further conversation on the subject of national affairs convinced me that he was a rank rebel.

We held a long conversation, on various topics. He informed me he had lived with the Indians fourteen years; was born in St. Louis, had an Indian wife, and several children of whom he was very proud; and he seemed to be perfectly satisfied with his mode of living.

I was very cautious in my words with him, lest he might prove to be a traitor; but in our conversation some Indian words escaped my lips, which, being overheard, rumor construed into mischief. What I had said was carried from lodge to lodge, increasing rather than diminishing, until it returned to the lodge where I was. The Indians, losing confidence in me, sent the young braves, at midnight, to the camp of the white man, to ascertain what had been said by me and my feelings toward them.

He assured the messengers that I was perfectly friendly, had breathed nothing but kindliness for them, was thoroughly contented, and there was no cause to imagine any evil.

This man trafficked and traded with the Indians, disposing of his goods in St. Louis and in eastern cities, and was then on his way to his home near the mouth of the Yellowstone River.

Early in the forenoon of the last day's travel my eager and anxious eyes beheld us nearing the fort. The Indians paused and dismounted to arrange their dress and see to the condition of their arms.

Their blankets and furs were adjusted; bows were strung and the guns carefully examined. They then divided into squads of fifty, several of these squads remaining in ambush among the hills for the purpose of intercepting any who might escape the anticipated massacre at the fort. The others then rode on toward the fort, bearing me with them.

A painfully startling sight (the last I was destined to see) here met my gaze. One of the warriors in passing thrust out his hand to salute me. It was covered by one of my husband's gloves, and the sight of such a memento filled me with inexpressible dread as to his fate. Nothing in the least way connected with him had transpired to throw any light upon his whereabouts, whether living or dead, since we had been so suddenly and cruelly separated. All was darkness and doubt concerning him.

Mr. Kelly had been a Union soldier, and happening to have his discharge papers with me at the time of my capture, I had been able to secrete them ever since, treasuring them because they had once belonged to him and contained his name.

Now, as we approached the place where his fate would be revealed to me, and, if he lived, we would meet once more, the appearance of that glove on the savage's hand was like a touch that awakened many chords, some to thrill with hope, some to jar painfully with fear.

In appearance I had suffered from my long estrangement from home life. I had been obliged to paint daily like the rest of my companions, and narrowly escaped tattooing by pretending to faint away each time I saw the implements for the operation.

During the journey, whenever an opportunity offered, I would use a handful of snow to cleanse my cheeks from savage adornment; and now, as we drew nearer to the fort, I could see the chiefs arranging themselves for effect. My heart beat faster and anticipation became so intense as to be painful.

Eight chiefs rode in the front, one leading my horse by the bridle, and the warriors rode in the rear. The cavalcade was imposing, and as we neared the fort, they raised their war song loud and wild into the still, wintry air. Then, as if in answer to its notes, the glorious flag of our country was run up and floated bravely forth on the breeze from the tall flagstaff within the fort.

My eyes caught the glad sight and my heart gave a wild bound of joy; something seemed to rise in my throat and choked my breathing. Everything was changed; the torture of suspense, the agony of fear, and dread of evil to come, all seemed to melt away like mist before the morning sunshine, when I beheld the precious emblem of liberty. How insignificant and contemptible by comparison were the flaunting Indian flags that had so long been displayed to me; and how my heart thrilled with a sense of safety and protection as I saw the roofs of the buildings within the fort covered by the brave men who composed that little garrison.

The precious emblem of liberty, whose beloved stars and stripes wafted proudly on air, seemed to beckon me to freedom and security; and as the fresh breeze stirred its folds, shining in the morning light, and caused them to wave lightly to and fro, they came like the smile of love and the voice of affection, all combined to warmly welcome me to home and happiness once more.

An Indian hanger-on at the fort had sauntered carelessly forward minutes earlier, as if actuated by curiosity, but in reality to convey intelligence about the state of the fort and its defenses.

Then the gate was opened and Major House, accompanied by several officers and an interpreter, received the chiefs who rode in advance.

Meanwhile, Captain Logan[4] (the officer of the day), a man whose kind and sympathetic nature did honor to his years and rank, approached me. My emotions were inexpressible now that I felt myself so nearly rescued. At last, they overcame me. I had borne grief and terror and privation, but the delight of being once more among my people was so overpowering that I almost lost the power of speech, and when I faintly murmured, "Am I free, indeed free?" Captain Logan's tears answered me as well as his scarcely uttered "Yes," for he realized what freedom meant to one who had tasted the bitterness of bondage and despair.

[4] John Logan was Captain, Company K of the Sixth Iowa Cavalry at Fort Sully.

As soon as the chiefs who accompanied me entered the gate of the fort, the commandant's voice thundered the order for them to be closed.

The Blackfeet were shut out, and I was beyond their power to recapture.

After a bondage lasting more than five months, during which I had endured every torture, I once more stood free among people of my own race, all ready to restore me to my husband's arms.

Three ladies residing at the fort received me, and cheerfully bestowed every care and attention which could add to my comfort and secure my recovery from the fatigues and distresses of my captivity.

XXII

My Husband Is Alive

AT FIRST, and for some time afterward, the effects of my life among the savages preyed upon my mind so as to injure its quiet harmony. I was ill at ease among my new friends, and they told me that my eyes wore a strangely wild expression, like those of a person who was constantly in dread of some unknown alarm.

Once more free and safe among civilized people, I looked back on the horrible past with feelings that defy description.

The thought of leaving this mortal tenement on the desert plain for the wolves to devour, and the bones to bleach under the summer sun and winter frosts had been painful indeed. Now, I knew that if the wearied spirit should leave its earthly home, the body would be cared for by kind Christian friends and tenderly laid beneath the grass and flowers, and my heart rejoiced therein.

Hunger, thirst, and long days of privation and suffering had been mine. No friendly voices cheered me on; all was silence and despair. But now the scene had changed and the all-wise Being, who is cognizant of every thought, knew the joy and gratitude of my soul.

203

True, during the last few weeks of my captivity, the Indians had done all in their power for me, all their circumstances and conditions would allow, and the women were very kind, but "their people were not my people," and I was detained a captive, far from home, friends, and civilization.

With Alexander Selkirk I could state, "Better dwell in the midst of alarms, than reign in this horrible place."[1]

Being young and possessed of great cheerfulness and elasticity of temper, I was enabled to bear trials which seemed almost impossible for human nature to endure and live.

Soon after my arrival at the fort, Captain Pell came and invited me to go to a trader's store to obtain a dress for myself. I needed it very much, having no clothing of my own to wear.

A kind lady, Mrs. Davis, accompanied me, and the sight that presented itself to my wondering eyes will never be erased from memory.

By the doorsteps, on the porches, and everywhere, were groups of hungry Indians of all sizes and both sexes, claiming to be friendly.

Some of them were covered with every conceivable kind of superficial clothing and adornment, and critically wanting in cleanliness, a peculiar trait among the Indians of the Northwest.

---

[1] Alexander Selkirk (1676–1721), a Scotsman, whose experiences as a castaway on a lonely island are said to have inspired the story of Robinson Crusoe.

There was the papoose, half-breeds of any number, a few absolutely nude, others wrapped slightly in bits of calico, a piece of buckskin, or fur.

Speculators, teamsters, and interpreters mingled with the soldiers of the garrison. Squaws with their brightly flashing shawls of red cloth receiving, in their looped-up blanket, the various articles of food such as sugar, rice, flour, and other things. Tall warriors bending over the same counter, purchasing tobacco, brass nails, knives, and glass beads while speaking a different language, and a stranger might well speculate which was the better prototype of tongues. The Cheyennes supplement their words with active and expressive gestures, while the Sioux more often use their tongues as well as their arms and fingers.

To all, whether half-breed, Indian, or white man, the gentlemanly trader gave kind and patient attention, while himself and the clerks seemed ready and capable of talking Sioux, French, or English, just as the case came to hand.

It was the twelfth of December when I reached the fort and the place seemed like heaven after the trials of savage life.

The officers and men were like brothers to me; and their tender sympathy united me to them in the strongest bonds of friendship, which not even death can sever.

A party and supper was made for my special benefit, and on New Year's morning I was serenaded

with cannon. Every attention and kindness was bestowed upon me; and to Dr. John Ball, post surgeon, I owe a debt of gratitude which mere words
can never express. He was my attendant physician
during my sojourn at the fort, and, as my physical
system had undergone very severe changes, I needed great care. Under his skillful treatment and patient attention, I soon recovered both health and
strength. I had been severely frozen on the last days
of my journey with the Indians to the fort.

Colonel Dimon, from Fort Rice, came to call on
me ere I left Fort Sully.[2] He was attended by an
escort of one hundred and eighty men.

He told me of his efforts to obtain my release,
and that he, with his men, had searched the Indian
village for me, but found no warriors there, as they
had already taken me to the fort. The Indian wom-
en had made him to understand by signs that the
"White Woman" had gone with the chiefs.

He said the Indians were so enraged about giving
me up that they killed three of his men and scalped

[2]Colonel Charles Augustus Ropes Dimon commanded the
First U.S. Volunteer Regiment at Fort Rice—a unit of "Galvanized Yankees," or paroled Confederate prisoners who
agreed to fight the Indians. A native of Massachusetts and a
protégé of General Benjamin Butler, Dimon had gone up
through the ranks from private and was regarded by his men
as the strictest of disciplinarians. Fort Rice was established
by General Sully in the summer of 1864 as a supply base for
his operations against the Sioux. It was on the right bank of
the Missouri, about ten miles north of the mouth of the Cannonball River.

Fort Rice, Dakota Territory
Courtesy State Historical Society of North Dakota

them, by orders from the chief, Ottawa, who was unable to do any service himself, being a cripple.

An Indian who killed one of the men fell dead in his lodge the same day, which frightened his people not a little; for, in their superstition, they deemed it a visitation of the Great Spirit for a wrong done.

Colonel Dimon did not forget about me, neither did he cease in his efforts in my behalf.

During all this time no tidings had been received by me concerning my husband. But one day, great commotion was occasioned in the fort by the announcement that the mail ambulance was on the way to the fort and would reach it in a few moments. An instant after, a soldier approached me saying: "Mrs. Kelly, I have news for you. Your husband is in the ambulance."

No person can have even a faint idea of the uncontrollable emotions which swept over me like an avalanche at that important and startling news. But it was not outwardly displayed. The heartstrings were stirred to their utmost depths but gave no sound. Trembling, quivering in their strong feeling they told nothing about the deep grief and joy intermingled there.

Mechanically, I moved around, awaiting the presence of my beloved and was soon folded onto his breast, where he held me with a grasp as if fearful of my being torn from him again.

All eyes present were suffused with tears. Soldiers and men, and the ladies who had been my friends all mingled their tears and prayers. Language fails to describe our meeting. For seven long months we had not beheld each other; the last time being on the terrible field of slaughter and death.

His personal appearance, oh! how changed! His face was very pale and his brown hair was sprinkled with gray. His voice was alone unchanged. Then he called my name and it never sounded so sweet before. His very soul seemed imbued with sadness because of our separation and the terrible events which caused it.

My first question was concerning my little Mary; for her fate had been veiled in mystery. He gave me the account of her burial—a sad and heartrending story, sufficient to chill the lightest heart.

XXIII

Sad Fate of Little Mary

THE READER will please go back with me to that fearful first night of my captivity, and to the moment when I put into execution the plan for dear little Mary's escape, which I prayed might result in her restoration to our friends.

It must have been something more than a vague hope of liberty to be lost or won that guided the feeble steps of the child back on the trail to a bluff overlooking the road where, weary from the fatigue and terror of a night passed alone on the prairie, she sat anxiously, awaiting the coming of friends.

Rescue was seemingly near, now that she had reached the great road and she knew that there would be a passing train of emigrants ere long.

It was in this situation she was seen by some passing soldiers, holding out her little trembling hands with eager joy and hope, begging them to save her.

It was a party of but three or four soldiers returning from Fort Laramie, where they had been to meet the paymaster. They had been pursued by Indians the day before; had also passed the scene of the destruction of our train; and believed the country swarming with Indians. Their apprehensions were, therefore, fully aroused, and fearing the little figure upon the distant bluff might be a decoy to lead them into ambush, hesitated to approach. There was a large ravine between, and it is not strange that their imagination should people it with lurking savages. However, they were about to cross and come to the relief of the little girl, when a party of Indians came in sight. They became convinced it was a decoy and turned and fled.

They returned to Deer Creek Station and related the circumstance. Mr. Kelly, arriving soon after, heard it and his heart sank within him at the description of the child, for he thought he recognized in it the form of our little Mary.

He applied to the officer in command for a detail of soldiers to go with him to search for her, but all entreaty and argument were in vain.

The agony that poor child endured as the soldiers went away and the war whoop of the savages rang upon her terrified soul is known only to God. Instead of the rescue and friends which in her trusting heart and innocent faith she had expected to find, fierce Indians stood before her, stringing their bows to take her life, thus to win another trophy marking the Indian murderer.

The whizzing arrows were sent into the body of the helpless child, and with the twang of the bowstrings, the delicate form of the heroic child lay stretched upon the ground and the bright angel spirit went home to rest in the bosom of its Father.

On the morning of the fourteenth, two days after

Mary was seen, Mr. Kelly succeeded in obtaining a squad of soldiers at the station and went out to search for the child. After a short march of eight miles, they discovered the mutilated remains of the murdered girl.

Three arrows had pierced her body, and the tomahawk and scalping knife had done their work. When discovered, her body lay with its little hands outstretched as if she had received, while running, the fatal arrows.

Extracting the arrows from the wounds and dividing her dress among the soldiers, then tenderly wrapping her in a winding sheet, Mr. Kelly had the sad satisfaction of smoothing the earth on the unconscious breast that had ceased to suffer. When this duty was performed, they left the little grave all alone, far from the happy home of her childhood and the brothers with whom she had played in her innocent joy.

Of all strange and terrible fates no one who had seen her gentle face in its loving sweetness, the joy and comfort of our hearts, would have predicted such a barbarous fate for her. But it was only the passage from death into life, from darkness into daylight, from doubt and fear into endless love and joy. Those little ones, whose spirits float upward from their downy pillows, amidst the tears and prayers of broken-hearted friends, are blest to enter in at heaven's shining gate, which lies as near little Mary's rocky, blood-stained pillow in the desolate waste as the palace of a king, and when she had once gained the great and unspeakable bliss of heaven, it must have blotted out the remembrance of the pain that won it, and made no price too great for such delight.

In the far-off land of Indian homes,
  Where western winds fan "hills of black,"
'Mid lovely flowers, and golden scenes,
  They laid our loved one down to rest.

Where brightest birds with silvery wings,
  Sing their sweet songs upon her grave,
And the moonbeam's soft and pearly beams
  With prairie grasses o'er it wave.

No simple stone e'er marks the spot
  Where Mary sleeps in dreamless sleep,
But the moaning wind with mournful sound,
  Doth nightly o'er it vigils keep.

The careless tread of savage feet,
  And the weary travelers pass it by,
Nor heed they her, who came so far
  In her youth and innocence to die.

But her happy spirit soared away
  To blissful climes above;
She found sweet rest and endless joy
  In her bright home of love.

XXIV

Events at Fort Laramie
after My Capture

IMMEDIATELY after Mr. Kelly reached Deer Creek, at the time of our capture, he telegraphed to Fort Laramie to announce the outbreak of the Indians and the capture of his wife.

Colonel Collins of the Eleventh Ohio Cavalry,[1] commandant of the military district, ordered two companies under Captain Shuman[2] and Captain Marshall, two brave and daring men, to pursue and rescue me, and chastise the savages in case of any attempted resistance.

However, a distance of one hundred miles lay between these forts, and the troops arrived too late for rescue. They continued their march, however, and after three days, returned unsuccessful.

---

[1]A lawyer, graduate of Amherst College and member of the Ohio Legislature from Hillsboro, Ohio, Lieutenant Colonel William O. Collins had in 1861 recruited and organized the companies that eventually became the Eleventh Ohio Volunteer Cavalry Regiment, stationed at Fort Laramie, with small garrisons along the Overland route for additional protection.

[2]With detachments of the Eleventh Ohio, Captain Jacob S. Shuman in the summer of 1864 built a new post twelve miles east of the present Wyoming-Nebraska border, known briefly as Camp Shuman, but renamed Fort Mitchell. He later settled in Sedalia, Missouri.

I am sad to relate that a young and undaunted officer, Lieutenant John Brown of the Eleventh Ohio
Volunteers[3] fell victim to savage cruelty in my behalf, for with a view of prospecting the neighborhood, he and Mr. Kelly left the main body with a
small squad of men in quest of the Indians. Coming
suddenly upon a band of warriors in their encampment, the brave Lieutenant indiscreetly ordered an
attack, but the men, sensing the futility of opposing
such numbers, fled, and left Mr. Kelly and the officer alone against the savages.

Becoming conscious of his dangerous situation,
he feigned friendship, addressing them in the usual
way, "*How koda?*" which means, "How do you do,
friend?"

But the Indians were not to be deceived, and sent
an arrow, causing him to fall from his horse and the
effects of which caused his death a few hours after
the confrontation.

He was immediately reported dead, and with all
the speed the men could command they pursued
his murderers; but the fresher horses of the savages
carried them off beyond their reach and the soldiers
were compelled to return in disappointment.

Brave young man! the ardent friend of Mr. Kelly
and the husband and father of an affectionate wife
and child, stricken down in his early manhood. We

[3]Twenty-three-year-old Lieutenant John Brown of Ohio
was killed July 21 at a site later known as Brown's Springs.
He had left a wife and child to enlist a year earlier.

would humbly lay a wreath of "immortelles" upon thy lonely grave.

After several expeditions in like manner which proved unsuccessful, Mr. Kelly offered a reward of nineteen horses, the money value of which was deposited with the commander of Fort Laramie, and it was circulated through all the Indian villages that upon my safe delivery the reward would be paid.

Every effort possible was made by my husband and his brothers to procure my rescue or ransom. No money or efforts were spared, and the long days of agonizing suspense to them were almost worse than death itself.[4]

The reward which had been offered for my ransom was eventually used to rescue another white woman, a Mrs. Ewbanks and her child, held by the Indians.[5]

The Indian Two Face and his son, having a desire

[4] According to Josiah Kelly, he spent $1,075 in attempting to ransom or rescue Fanny and in escorting her home. He also unsuccessfully dunned the Federal Government for $50,000 to cover, in his words, "Damages for my wife's being made prisoner and Slave and Suffering Starvation Privation disease frozen limbs and being tormented and suffering all the abuse that those savage devils could invent for five months." Josiah Kelly's affidavit (1866), is exhibit "A" in Fanny Kelly Petition (1868), House Committee on Appropriations Papers, 40th Cong., RG 233, National Archives.

[5] Mrs. Lucinda Eubanks (sometimes spelled Ewbanks) and her infant daughter had been captured by the Oglala Sioux raiders on the Little Blue River in Kansas and spent fourteen difficult months in captivity prior to their release in the spring of 1865.

Fort Laramie, Wyoming Territory
(As Sketched in 1863 by C. Moellman,
a Bugler with the Eleventh Ohio Volunteer Cavalry)
Courtesy American Heritage Center, University of Wyoming

to enhance their fortunes, paid a small amount to the Indians who held her. Then taking her with them, set out for Fort Laramie. When they arrived within a few miles of the fort, Mrs. Ewbanks and her child were left with the son and some others, while Two Face preceded them to arrange the terms of ransom.

The commander agreed to the price, and on the following day Mrs. Ewbanks and her child were brought in—the Indians thinking it made no difference which white woman it was. This was several months after my capture.

Instead of paying the price, the commandant seized the Indians and confined them in the guardhouse to await trial for the murder of the men and the stealing of women and children. The testimony of Mrs. Ewbanks was proof positive. The Indians then confessed to their crimes and were executed the following May.[6]

When crossing the North Platte River, five miles below the fort, Mrs. Ewbanks suffered intensely, her child being bound to her back, and she holding on to a log bound by a rope fastened to the saddle of the Indian's horse.

The chief passed over easily, but mother and

[6]Two of the Oglalas, Two Face and Black Foot, were hanged by chains. Some reports insist that both were friendly to whites, had bought the woman and child at their expense from their captors and brought them to surrender willingly, only to be executed on the orders of a drunken commander, Colonel Thomas O. Moonlight.

child were nearly frozen to death by clinging and struggling among masses of broken ice, and protected only by a thin, light garment.

Mr. Kelly sent deputations of Indians with horses to the Indian villages, with letters to me which were never delivered. They were not true to their trust, but would come to see me without giving me the messages, then return with the declaration that I could not be found.

My husband would furnish a complete outfit for an Indian, which cost about four hundred dollars, and send him to find me; but the Indian cared only for the money; he would never return.

Having despaired of accomplishing anything further toward my rescue at Fort Laramie, he left for Leavenworth to obtain help from citizens there; to get permission of the commander of the division to raise an independent company for my release.

There he met with his brother, General Kelly,[7] who had just returned from the South and had received a letter from me, acquainting him with my freedom.

Mr. Kelly would not at first be convinced, but, after being shown the letter, he said, "Yes, I know that is Fanny's writing, but it cannot be possible;" yet he was soon on his way to Dakota Territory.

---

[7] Josiah's brother, William Harrison Kelly (1836–99), was mustered out of the Fifth Kansas Volunteer Cavalry as a captain. Later, in 1865, he was appointed brigadier general in the Kansas militia.

Who can tell his varied emotions during that long and wearisome journey, when, at the end, hope held out to him the cup of joy which, after the long suffering of months, he was about to drink. Let only those judge who have been separated from the dearest on earth, and whose fate was involved in mysterious silence, more painful than if the pallid face rested beneath the coffin lid.

XXV

Sadness and Joy

FORT SULLY was garrisoned by three companies of the Sixth Iowa Cavalry, and I should be recreant to every sense of justice did I not more particularly express my deep gratitude to them all—officers and men—for the delicate, more than brotherly, kindness shown to me during my stay of two months among them.

They had fought gallantly during that summer and punished severely the Indians who held me captive; and though my sufferings at the time were increased tenfold thereby, I believe the destitute condition of the Indians had much to do with my final restoration to freedom. Had there been plenty of food in the Indian villages, none would have gone to Fort Sully to make a treaty.

On each of the two evenings we remained at the fort after my husband's arrival, we were honored with a "feast," in marked contrast with those I had attended while with the savages. Stewed oysters relished better than stewed dog, and the abundance of other good things with the happy-looking, kind, sympathetic faces of my own people around the board filled me with a feeling of almost heavenly content.

221

Mr. Harry Chatterton[1] presided at the first, and in a feeling manner expressed the delight and satisfaction his comrades and himself experienced in this hour of our reunion:

"Sweet is this dream—divinely sweet—
No dream! no fancy! that you meet;
Tho' silent grief has shadowed o'er
To crush your love—it had no power—
Tho' long divided you've met once more
To tell your toils and troubles o'er;
Renew the pledge of other days,
And walk in sweet and pleasant ways

"May the good Father of mercies ever protect and bless you; make the sun of happiness to brightly shine upon you, and may it never again be dimmed by stern misfortune! is the earnest and heartfelt wish of every person in this fort today."

How many affectionate and generous natures are among us, whom we can never appreciate until some heavy cloud drops down upon us, and they with their cheerful words and kind acts assist us to rise, and in hours of joy they are ready to grasp us by the hand and welcome us to happiness?

Anxious for a reunion with our friends and to be once more with my dear mother, we bade farewell to those who had shown us so much kindness and

[1] Harry R. Chatterton, a non-commissioned officer in Co. B, Sixth Iowa Volunteer Cavalry, was with the Sully campaigns and was at Fort Sully when Fanny was brought in.

attention, and commenced our journey at daylight to prevent the Indians, many of whom remained about the fort, knowing of my departure as I was in constant dread of recapture.

Fort Sully is on the Missouri River, three hundred miles from Sioux City by land, which distance we traveled in an ambulance. At all the military posts, stations, and towns through which we passed, all—military and civilians—seemed to vie with each other in kindness and attention. Those living in frontier towns know what the nature of the Indian is, and could most heartily sympathize with one who had suffered from captivity among them.

At Yankton, I received particularly kind attention from Mrs. Ash of the Ash Hotel, who also gave me the information, elsewhere written, regarding the fate of Mrs. Dooley and Mrs. Wright.[2] Here, also, I met a number of the Sixth Iowa Cavalry, the gallant regiment to which I owe so much. Dr. Bardwell,[3] a surgeon of the regiment stationed at Fort Sully at the time the Blackfeet came in to make a

[2] Julia Wright was another of the victims of the Lake Shetek attack by White Lodge's band of Santee Sioux. She and her three children were captured. One daughter, an infant, had its brains dashed out by its captor. Julia, a strong, intelligent woman of spirit persevered and after less than two months she and her remaining children were released thanks to Charles Galpin and his associates. Gray, "The Santee Sioux and the Settlers at Lake Shetek," *Montana*, XXV (Winter, 1975), pp. 46–47, 51, 53.

[3] Thomas S. Bardwell, Assistant Surgeon of the Sixth Iowa Cavalry, was from Marion.

treaty and were sent off after me, and who, I had previously been informed, was active in measures tending to my release, was stationed at Yankton, and manifested the kindness of his heart in many different ways.

At Sioux City, Council Bluffs, and St. Joseph, crowds of visitors flocked to see the white woman who had been a captive with the Indians, and I was compelled to answer many questions. From St. Joe we made all haste for Leavenworth, Kansas, where I was received by friends and relatives as one risen from the dead.

At last, we reached our old home in Geneva; the home from which we had departed only several months before, lured to new fields by the brightest hopes of future prosperity. Alas! what disappointments had fallen to our lot! But soon I was clasped in my dear mother's arms, and all my sorrows were swallowed up in the joy of the reunion.

On the morning of our departure for the plains she said (while tears of sorrow filled her eyes) that she felt as though it was our final farewell. Her fears were agonizing in my behalf. She appeared to have a presentiment of evil—a dark, portentous cloud hung over my head, she felt, that would burst upon me, and scatter dismay and grief—which too well was realized in the days that followed.

I endeavored to cheer her with hope, and smilingly assured her that as soon as the Pacific Railroad was completed, I should visit my home and her; and though many miles might yet separate us, we still would be one in heart. Furthermore, the facilities for traveling were becoming so easy and rapid, we could not be separated for any great length of time. But her sad heart refused to be comforted. A mother's unchanging love—stronger than death, faithful under every circumstance, and clinging with tenacity to the child of her affection—could not part with me without a pang of anguish, which was increased tenfold when the news of my capture reached her.

Gradually she sank under this heavy affliction; health rapidly gave way, and for three long months she lay helpless, moaning and bewailing the loss of her children. Scarcely had she aroused from the terrible stupor and grief caused by the news of my brother's death from poison while a soldier in the Union army, when this new and awful sorrow of my captivity came like a whirlwind upon her frail and fainting spirit.[4]

But God is good. In His great mercy He spared us both to meet again, and a letter from my hand telling her of my safety reached her in due time. Now in each other's fond embrace we were once more folded.

Oh! happy hour! Methinks the angels smiled in their celestial abodes when they witnessed that dear mother's joy.

[4] Henry Wiggins was a member of the Ninth Kansas Cavalry and died on January 2, 1863, at the age of nineteen, probably of disease, not poison.

The reader naturally supposes that here my narrative should conclude; that, restored to husband, mother, and friends, my season of sorrow must be over. But not so. Other trials were in store for me, and even fortified as I was by past tribulation, I sank almost despairingly under this affliction. Nor was I yet done with the Indians.

Anxious to again establish a home, we left Geneva and went to Shawneetown where we prospered. Soon better prospects took us further west; we went to Ellsworth, a new town just staked out near the western line of Kansas.[5] I was the first woman who located there. We lived in our wagon for a time, then built a hotel and were prospering when fears of the Indians again harassed us.

The troops at Fort Harker, three miles east of Ellsworth, had been out under General Hancock,[6] pursuing Indians so as to punish them for murders and depredations committed along the line of the Pacific Railroad. The soldiers soon located an Indian camp and destroyed it, inflicting a severe chastisement. We knew this act would so exasperate the

[5]Shawneetown was the site of the old Shawnee Mission, on the western edge of what is now Kansas City. Ellsworth was located in 1867 sixty miles west of Abilene on the Kansas Pacific Railroad building westward, and for a time became an important trail town for Texas cattle.

[6]Major General Winfield Scott Hancock, hero of Churubusco, Spottsylvania and Gettysburg, and a future presidential candidate, led a large expedition into western Kansas in the spring of 1867 to over-awe the Indians with a show of force that was only partially successful.

Indians that the situation of the exposed settlements would become one of great danger; and after my experience, a terrible dread of again falling into their hands intensified my apprehensions for our safety.

The scouts, Jack Harvey and "Wild Bill," were constantly on the lookout, and eagerly would we look toward the hills for anyone who could give us news, and when they came from the front would speedily gather around them with anxious faces and listening ears.

Meanwhile the population of Ellsworth had rapidly increased and military companies were formed for protection. Thus we lived in a continual state of alarm, until, at last, one night the signal was given that the Indians were approaching. Every man flew to his post, and the women and children fled to the places of refuge that had been prepared for them: an ironclad house and an underground dugout. I fled to the latter place, where about fifty others had congregated. Among them were three young men who, we had just recently learned, were the sole survivors of a large family—father, mother, and two sisters—murdered and horribly mutilated in the Minnesota massacres.

The Indians were repulsed, but they continued to harass us and threaten the town, so it became necessary to request military protection. In due time a number of troops arrived and this imparted a feeling of security.

But Ellsworth was doomed to a more terrible scourge, if possible, than the Indians had threatened to be. The newly arrived troops were recently from the South, and very soon after their arrival, cholera broke out among them, then quickly spread among the citizens, creating a terrible panic. The pestilence was most destructive, sweeping before it old and young, and of all classes.

My husband fell a victim to the disease.

On the twenty-eighth day of July, 1867 a violent attack of this terrible disease carried him off, and in the midst of peril and cares I was left a mourning, desolate widow.

Being in delicate health, I was forced to flee to the East. On my way I stopped off at St. George,[7] where one week later my little one was ushered into this world of sorrow.

The people were panic stricken with regard to the cholera, and when I went there, they were afraid to receive me into their homes. Consequently, I repaired to a small cabin on the outskirts of the town, and my adopted son[8] and I remained there alone for several days.

A young lady, Miss Baker, called on me in great sympathy, saying she was not afraid of cholera and would stay with me until after my confinement.

[7] The oldest settlement in Pottawatomie County, St. George was located on the Kansas River, just east of the town of Manhattan.

[8] Apparently this was the son of Fanny's sister, and the brother of little Mary. He was not long with Mrs. Kelly.

I was very thankful for her kindness, and after the fear was over with the people, every attention that humanity could suggest was given me; but, alas! my heart was at home, and so deep were my yearnings, the physician declared it impossible for me to recover until I did go home.

The physician who attended me went to Ellsworth to see if it was prudent for me to return. Soon a letter arrived bidding me to come, as the cholera had disappeared.

Oh! how changed was that home! The voice that had ever been as low, sweet music to my ear was hushed forever; the eye that had always met mine with smiling fondness was closed to light and me, and the hand so often grasped in tender love was palsied in death! Mr. Kelly, the noble, true, and devoted husband, my loved companion, the father of my newly born child was gone. Oh! how sad that word! My heart was overwhelmed with grief, and that did its work, for it prostrated me on a bed of illness nigh unto death.

Dr. McKennon faithfully attended me during my illness, and as I was recovering, he was seized by a severe sickness which proved to be fatal.

He was anxious to see me before he died, and desired assistance that he might be taken downstairs for the purpose.

His attendants allowed him to do so, but he fainted in the attempt and was laid on the floor until he recovered, then raised and placed on the sofa.

I was then led into the room and seated myself beside him. He grasped my hand, exclaiming: "My friend, do not leave me. I have a brother in New York"—but his lips soon stiffened in death and he was unable to utter more.

It was a severe shock to my nervous system, already prostrated by trouble and illness, and I greatly missed his attention and care.

No relative or friend was near to lay his weary head upon the pillow; but we laid him to rest in the burial ground of Ellsworth with saddened hearts and great emotion.

In the spring I went to the end of the road further west with an excursion party, to a place called Sheridan.[9] Upon our return we stopped at Fort Hays where I came upon two Indians who recognized me, and I also knew them. As we conversed, I learned they had a camp in the vicinity and were skulking around, reconnoitering. They seemed well treated here and very liberally dealt with. They inquired where I lived and I told them way off, near to the rising sun.

The next morning when the train left town, the Indian band, riding on horseback, jumped the ditch and looked into the windows of the cars, hoping to see me.

They told the people that I belonged to them,

[9]In 1868 Sheridan was the end of the track for the Kansas Pacific railroad—with further construction temporarily suspended the town teemed with rough and ready characters.

and they would take my papoose and me way off to their own country; we were their property and must go with them.

It was supposed that if I had been in the cars the Indians would have attempted to take the train.

XXVI

Fates of Other Captives

SOME FEW weeks after the events just related, I received a note from a stranger requesting me to call on her at the dwelling of a hunter, where she was stopping. Her name was Elizabeth Blackwell, and she had emigrated with her parents from England. They had become proselytes of the ruling prophet of Salt Lake City, where they remained until Elizabeth's father took another wife. This created trouble; words ensued, soon followed by blows, and Elizabeth, in endeavoring to protect her mother, was struck by her brute of a father with a knife and one of her eyes was destroyed.

Being both discouraged and brokenhearted, the wretched mother and daughters (for Elizabeth had two sisters) resolved to leave their home. They wandered into the mountains, and having no place of shelter, all perished from the cold, except Elizabeth who was found by the Indians nearly frozen to death. They lifted her up and carried her to camp where they gave her every attention requisite for restoration.

She remained with the Indians until she was able to go east, where she underwent the severe operation of having both legs amputated above the knee.

232

The treatment received from the Indians so attached her to them that she prefers to live a forest life, and when she gave me her narrative, she was on her way from the States to her Indian home.

Her father soon wearied of his Mormon wife and escaped to the Rocky Mountains, where he became a noted highwayman. Hearing of Elizabeth's residence among the Indians, he visited her and gave her a large sum of money. The fate of his family had great effect on him, and remorse drove him to desperation.

The husband of Elizabeth took his second wife and Elizabeth's child from Salt Lake to Cincinnati, where they now live.

She was twenty-six years old when I conversed with her, a lady of intelligence, and once possessed more than ordinary beauty.

She had just received the news of her father's death. He was killed near Fort Dodge, Kansas.

Elizabeth related to me many acts of cruelty she had witnessed among the savages, one of which was to the following effect:

A woman, who had been captured from a train, was brought into the Indian camp on horseback and the Indian who was attempting to lift her from the horse was shot in the act by her own hand. This so enraged the savages that they cut her body in gashes, filled them with powder and then set fire to it.

The sight of the woman's terrible suffering was too much for Elizabeth to endure and she begged the savages to put a merciful end to the victim at once, which accordingly was done.

But although Elizabeth saw many heartless acts—many terrible scenes—still she had a kindly feeling toward the Indians for they had saved her from a horrible death by starvation and exposure, and had been very tender with her. Conversely, she was somewhat embittered toward the white people on account of the sufferings and treatment she received from them.

A short time later, General Sully invited me to Fort Harker to see two white captive children, a girl of fourteen and a boy of six. They had been captured two years before and the account of their treatment given me by the girl was anything but favorable. The boy was as wild as a deer.

In January, 1868, two other children were captured in the State of Texas by the Kiowa Indians. They were girls, aged five and three years. Their parents and all the known relatives had been murdered. The children had been recently recovered from the Indians and were in the care of J. H. Leavenworth, United States Indian Agent. Having no knowledge of their parentage, they were named Helen and Heloise Lincoln.

Another Texas family was taken by the Indians, their beautiful home destroyed, and all killed with the exception of the mother and three daughters.

Their name was Boxx. The ages of the children were respectively eighteen, fourteen, and ten, and they were allowed to be together for a time, but afterward were separated.

They experienced great cruelties. The youngest was compelled to stand on a bed of live coals in order to torture the mother and sisters.

Lieutenant Hesselberger, the noble and brave officer, whose name will live forever in the hearts of the captives he rescued, heard of this family, and with a party of his brave men, went immediately to the Indian village and offered a reward for the captives, which at first was declined, but he at length succeeded in purchasing the mother and one girl and afterward procured the release of the others.[1]

Lieutenant Hesselberger braved death in so doing, and his only reward is the undying gratitude of those who owe their lives to his self-sacrificing, humane devotion and courage.

In the fall of 1868 the Indians commenced depredations on the frontier of Kansas, and after many serious outbreaks, destroying homes and murdering

[1] Fanny Kelly's memory and spelling differs only slightly from the accepted record which is as follows: A band of Kiowas under Santana attacked the James Box family in Cooke County, Texas, in the summer of 1866, killing Box and capturing his wife, Mary, and their four daughters, the youngest an infant who died in a fall onto the rocks. Mrs. Box, Margaret, aged 17, Josephine, aged 13, and Ida, aged 7, endured brutal captivity for about ten weeks before being ransomed as a result of Hesselberger's negotiations. Lonnie J. White, "White Women Captives of Southern Plains Indians, 1866–1875," *Journal of the West,* VIII (July, 1969), pp. 330–34.

settlers, the Governor issued a call for volunteers to assist General Sheridan in protecting the settlers and punishing the Indians.[2] Among those who volunteered was my youngest brother[3] and many of my old schoolmates and friends from Geneva, who related to me the following incidents, which are fully substantiated by General Sheridan and others.

Mrs. Morgan, a most accomplished and beautiful bride, and Miss White, a well-educated young lady, were both taken from their homes by the Indians.[4] They were living on the Republican River.

During their captivity they suffered much from the inclemency of the weather, and it was March before they were rescued by General Sheridan.

[2] A West Point officer renowned for his toughness in the Civil War, Major General Philip H. Sheridan in 1867 added the innovation of winter campaigns to Plains warfare and brought an unremittingly harsh offensive against the Kiowas, Comanche, and Southern Cheyennes.

[3] William J. Wiggins was a six-month enlistee in the Kansas Volunteers, ten companies of which were part of George Custer's command in the western Kansas campaign during the winter of 1868–69. General Phil Sheridan directed the entire operation.

[4] Mrs. Anna Belle Morgan was taken captive by Sioux in October, 1868, in Ottawa County, Kansas, even though she emptied a revolver at her assailants. Subsequently she was traded to the Cheyennes and in March, 1869, was released after Custer threatened to summarily execute three captured Cheyenne chiefs. Eighteen-year-old Sarah C. White was captured and her father killed by Cheyennes, August 13, 1868, at their home on Granny Creek in Cloud County, Kansas—the same Indians who held Anna Morgan. She was also released when Custer promised an eye for an eye.

The troopers, all Kansas boys, spent all winter among the mountains, endeavoring to protect the wild frontier. They suffered great privation, being obliged at times to live on the meat of mules, and often needing food. All honors should be granted to these self-sacrificing men, who braved the cold and fought off hunger in the mountains to protect the settlers on the frontier.

A Mrs. Blynn, whose maiden name was Harrington, of Franklin County, Kansas, was married at the age of nineteen and started with her young husband for the Pacific coast. She was taken prisoner by the Indians and suffered terrible brutality.[5]

About that time, the savages had become troublesome on the plains, attacking every wagon train, killing men and capturing women. But the train in which Mr. Blynn and his wife traveled was supposed to be very strong, and able to repel any attack made upon them, should there be any such trouble.

Mrs. Blynn had a presentiment of evil—of the fate of their unfortunate company and her own dark impending destiny in a dream, the realization of which proved too true.

[5]Mrs. Clara Blynn and her two-year-old son, Willie, were captured by Cheyennes in an attack on a civilian wagon train on the Santa Fe Trail between Fort Lyon, Colorado, and Fort Dodge in October, 1868. Two months later, as an expedition headed by Colonel Custer attacked the Indian camp on the Washita, Clara Blynn and Willie were killed by their captors.

When she related her dream to her husband, he tried to laugh away her superstitious fears and prevent its impression on her mind.

It was not many days after that a large number of warriors of the Sioux tribe were seen in the distance, and the people of the train arranged themselves in a shape for attack.

The Indians, seeing this preparation and fearing a powerful resistance, fired a few shots and with yells of rage and disappointment went off.

Within the succeeding days the travelers saw Indians, but they did not come near enough to make trouble.

Confident of neither disturbance nor hindrance to their journey, the happy emigrants journeyed on fearless (comparatively) of the savages and boasting of their power.

But the evil hour at last approached. When the column had reached Sand Creek and was in the act of crossing, the wild yells of Indians suddenly fell upon their ears, and at once a band of Cheyennes charged down upon them.

Two wagons had already got into the stream, and instead of hastening the others across, thus putting the creek between themselves and their pursuers, the whites drove the two back out of the water and entangled in the others, throwing everything into confusion. This confusion is just what the Indians like, and they began whooping, shouting, and firing furiously in order to stampede the livestock.

In five minutes all was accomplished; all the animals, except for those well-fastened to the wagons, were dashing over the prairie. The Indians began to circle around and fired a volley of bullets and arrows. Mr. Blynn was killed at the second fire while standing before the wagon which carried his wife and child.

"God help them!" was all he said as he fired his rifle at the Indians for the last time. Then he fell down dead.

The men returned the fire for awhile, then fled, leaving the wounded, their wagons, and the women and children in the hands of the relentless victors.

Santana, who led the band, sprang in first, followed by his braves, whom he ordered to let the cowardly palefaces run away without pursuit.

The dead and wounded were scalped, and the women and children taken captive. All were treated with brutal conduct; and having secured all the plunder they could, the savages set fire to every wagon, and with the horses they had taken from the train, set out in the direction of their villages.

Mrs. Blynn's child, Willie, two years old, cried very much, which so enraged Santana that he seized him by the heels and was poised to dash out his brains, but the poor mother in her agony sprang forward, caught the child, and fought so bravely with the infuriated murderer that he laughed and told her to keep it; for he feared she would fret if he killed it.

Mounted on a pony, her child in her arms, she endeavored to please her savage captor by appearing satisfied, dwelling on the hope that some event would occur whereby she might be rescued and restored to her friends. It was for her darling child that she endeavored to keep up her heart and resolve to live.

Upon their arrival at Santana's village, Mrs. Blynn was separated from the seven who were taken. Group after group dropped away from the main body, taking with them the women whom they had as prisoners.

Her hardships soon commenced. For a day or two she was fed sufficiently; but afterward all that she had to eat she got from the squaws in the same lodge with her; and as they were jealous of her, they often refused to give her anything, either for herself or Willie.

An Indian girl, in revenge for the murder of her best friend by Santana, became a spy for General Sheridan and endeavored by every means in her power to rescue Mrs. Blynn from the grasp of these savages, but her efforts were unsuccessful. She was a true friend to the unfortunate lady, giving her food and endeavoring to cheer her with the promise of rescue and safe deliverance.

The squaws abused her shamefully in the absence of Santana, burning her with sharp sticks and splinters of resinous wood and inflicting the most excruciating tortures upon her. Her face, breasts, and limbs were one mass of wounds. Her precious little one was taken by the hair of the head and punished with a stick before her helpless gaze.

Mrs. Blynn, previous to this torture, had written a letter to the general commanding the department, whoever he might be, and sent it by the Indian girl.

Here is a copy of this letter, which is sufficient to draw tears from the eye of anyone who may read it.

Kiowah Village, on The Washita River
Saturday, November 7, 1868

Kind Friend:

Whoever you may be, if you will only buy us from the Indians with ponies or anything, and let me come and stay with you until I can get word to my friends, they will pay you well; and I will work for you also, and do all I can for you.

If it is not too far to this village, and you are not afraid to come, I pray you will try.

The Indians tell me, as near as I can understand, they expect traders to come, to whom they will sell us. Can you find out by the bearer, and let me know if they are white men? If they are Mexicans, I am afraid they will sell us into slavery in Mexico.

If you can do nothing for me, write, for God's sake! to W. T. Harrington, Ottawa, Franklin County, Kansas—my father. Tell him we are with the Kiowahs, or Cheyennes; and they say when the white men make peace we can go home.

Tell him to write to the Governor of Kansas about it, and for them to make peace. Send this to him, please.

We were taken on October 9th, on the Arkansas, below Fort Lyon. My name is Mrs. Clara Blynn. My little boy, Willie Blynn, is two years old.

Do all you can for me. Write to the Peace Commissioners to make peace this fall. For our sake do all you can, and God will bless you for it!

If you can let me hear from you, let me know what you think about it. Write to my father. Send him this.

Mrs. R. F. Blynn

P. S.—I am as well as can be expected, but my baby, my darling, darling little Willie, is very weak. O, God! help him! Save him, kind friend, even if you cannot save me. Again, good-by.

Mrs. Blynn passed her time in drudgery, hoping against hope up to the morning of the battle, when General Sheridan's gallant soldiers, under the command of General Custer,[6] came charging with loud huzzahs upon the village.

Black Kettle's camp was the first attacked, though all the village was, of course, aroused.

The heart of Mrs. Blynn must have beat wildly, mingling with hope and dread, when she heard the noise and firing, and saw the United States soldiers charging upon her captors.

Springing forward, she exclaimed: "Willie, Willie, saved at last!" but the words were scarce on her lips, ere the tomahawk of the revengeful Santana was buried in her brain; and in another instant little Willie was in the grasp of the monster and his head dashed against a tree; then, lifeless, he was thrown upon the dying mother's breast, whose arms instinctively closed around the dead baby as though she would protect him to the last moment of her life.

[6]George Armstrong Custer, the "Boy General" of the Civil War, now a lieutenant colonel in the Seventh Cavalry, played a prominent part in the Hancock campaign against the Indians on the plains.

General Sheridan and his staff, in searching for the bodies of Major Elliott and his comrades, found them among the white soldiers and they were tenderly carried to Fort Cobb, where, in a grave outside the stockade, mother and child lie sleeping peacefully, their once bruised spirits having joined the loved husband and father in the land where captivity is unknown.

Surely, if heaven is gained through the sorrows of earth, this little family will enjoy the brightest scenes of the celestial world.

XXVII

False Friends and Compensation

MR. KELLY'S sudden death, my own sickness, and the scourge of cholera, all coming at one time, proved disastrous to me in a pecuniary way. I was defrauded in every way, even to the robbing of my husband's body of the sum of five hundred dollars on the day of his death. However, I finally disposed of the remnant of property left and started for Wyoming, where lived the only persons beside myself who survived the attack on our train. They had prospered, and in a spirit of kindness, as I then thought, invited and prevailed on me to share their home.[1]

It proved a most disastrous move for me. My leisure hours, since my release from captivity, had been devoted to preparing for publication, in book form, a narrative of my experience and adventures among the Indians, and it was completed. Then the manuscript was surreptitiously taken and a garbled, imperfect account of my captivity issued as the experience of my false friend, who, by the aid of an

[1]These were William and Sarah Larimer, traveling companions who shared the attack at the Little Box Elder Creek, and who then established themselves at Sherman Station in the retail and photography business.

244

Indian, escaped after a duration of but a single day and night.

I remained in Wyoming one year, then started for Washington, resolved to present a claim to the Government for losses sustained at the hands of the Indians. I knew what difficulties beset my path, but duty to my child urged me on, and I was not without some hope of success.

After learning of my captivity through Captain Fisk, President Lincoln had issued orders to the different military commanders that my freedom from the Indians must be purchased at any price; and my sad story was well known to the then existing authorities when I arrived in Washington.

President Grant, learning through a friend from Colorado of my presence, sent for me and assured me of his warmest sympathy. He was cognizant of what had already transpired relative to me, and told me the papers were on file in the War Department in charge of General Sherman.[2]

In presenting my claim many difficulties had to be encountered; but members of Congress, realizing that some compensation was due me, and understanding the delay that would result from a direct application to the Indian Bureau, introduced a bill which appropriated five thousand dollars to me for

[2]General William T. Sherman, a Union hero of the Civil War, was from 1866 to 1869 in command of the Division of the Missouri, which included all of the Great Plains. From 1869 to 1884 he was General of the Army.

valuable services I gave the Government in saving Captain Fisk's train from destruction, and by timely warning saving Fort Sully from pillage and its garrison from being massacred. This was handled without my having any knowledge of it until the bill had passed both houses of Congress and become law.[3]

During my stay in Washington, Red Cloud arrived with a delegation of chiefs and head warriors from the different tribes of the Dakota or Sioux nation. They all recognized me as having been with their people, and seemed rejoiced at our meeting.

Some of the good Christian people of the city extended to the Indians, through me, an invitation to attend church one Sabbath, which I made known to Red Cloud. I told him of the great organ and the fine music they would hear, and of the desire the good people had to benefit their souls.

Red Cloud replied with dignity that he did not have to go to the big house to talk to the Great Spirit, he could sit in his tipi or room and the Great Spirit would listen. The Great Spirit was not where the big music was. No, he would not go.

None of the Indians accepted the invitation, but some of the squaws went, escorted to the church in elegant carriages; but they soon left in disgust. The dazzling display of stylish dresses, the beautiful church, and the "big music"—none of these had interest for them, if unaccompanied by a feast.

[3]Fanny's typeset petition to Congress is reproduced in its entirety on pages 335-37 in the Appendix.

I attended several of the councils held with the Indians. At one of them, Red Cloud addressed Secretary Cox and Commissioner Parker[4] in a lengthy speech on the subject of his grievances, in which he referred to me as follows. Pointing me out to the Secretary and Commissioner, he said:

"Look at that woman; she was captured by Silver Horn's party. I wish you to pay her what her captors owe her. I am a man true to what I say, and want to keep my promise. I speak for all my nation. The Indians robbed that lady there, and through your influence I want her to be paid out of the first money due to us." Placing his finger first upon the breast of the Secretary and then of the Commissioner, as if to add emphasis to what he was about to say, he added, "Pay her out of our money; do not give the money into any but her own hands; then the right one will get it."

In one of my interviews with the chiefs, Red Cloud, Spotted Tail, and others desired me to get up a paper setting forth my claims against their people, and they would sign it. I accordingly made out a bill of items and presented it to them, with my affidavit and a statement setting forth the circumstances of capture and robbery, which was fully explained to them by their interpreter.

[4] A former Union general and governor of Ohio, Jacob D. Cox was Secretary of the Interior, 1869–70. Ely Parker, a mixed-blood Seneca of New York, fought with Grant at Vicksburg, and later became Grant's secretary and in 1869 Commissioner of Indian Affairs.

This document the chiefs representing the different bands signed readily. It is inserted elsewhere, with other documents corroborative of the truth of this narrative. It is also signed by another delegation of chiefs I met in New York.

With this last interview with the delegation of Indians I met in New York ends, I trust forever, my experience with Indians. The preparation of the manuscript for this plain, simple narrative of facts has not been without its pangs. It has seemed as if with the narration of each incident, I was living over again the fearful life I led while a captive; and often have I laid aside the pen to get rid of the feelings which possessed me. But my task is completed; and with the ending of this chapter, I hope to lay aside forever all regretful remembrances of my captivity, and looking only at the silvery lining to be found in every cloud, enjoy the happiness which everyone may find in childlike trust in Him who ordereth all things well.

XXVIII

General Sully's Expedition

DURING the summer of 1864, and while I was a prisoner with the Indians, an expedition composed of Iowa and Minnesota volunteers with a few independent companies of Nebraska and Dakota men and one company of friendly Indians of various tribes started from Fort Sully. Instructions from the War Department gave it the double purpose of escorting a large emigrant train safely through the Indian country on the way to Idaho, and, if possible, to inflict such punishment on the hostile bands they might meet as would make them willing to sue for peace.

The expedition was commanded by General Alfred Sully, a brave, skillful officer, and veteran Indian fighter, having spent the best part of twenty-five years' service on the frontier. He was a captain of infantry under General Harney in his memorable campaign of 1857, and was present at the battle of Ash Hollow, where Harney surprised a large band of Indians who were slaughtered indiscriminately. The punishment inflicted made the name of General Harney a terror to the Indians, and at the same time, brought upon his head the execration of thin-skinned philanthropists, who thought savages—the

249

"noble red men" as they imagined—should be conquered only by a sugarplum and rosewater policy.

For many interesting particulars of this expedition, and its bearing upon some of the incidents of my captivity and final ransom, I am indebted to the correspondence of one who was a member of the expedition, written to his family during its progress.

The first day's march carried the command to the Cheyenne River where the topographical engineer, to whom I have referred, was killed. His fate was sad, indeed. As an officer in the regular army, he served with distinction in the South during the rebellion, participating in over fifty battles and passing through all without a wound. He was captured by the rebels, paroled, and sent to join General Sully's expedition to make a topographical survey of the country.

Having faced danger on many a well-contested field, he held the Indian in complete contempt and roamed the country along the line of march with reckless indifference to danger.

A short time before reaching the place where the command intended to go into camp, Captain Fielner started in advance, accompanied by only one man, a half-breed. Reaching the river, they dismounted, and were about fastening their horses to graze near a grove of wild plum trees, when two Indians stepped out, and one of them shot Captain Fielner, the ball from his rifle passing through both arms and the breast. The advance guard arriving soon after sent back word to General Sully, who ordered the company of Dakota Cavalry to deploy and occupy so much of the country as to make it impossible for the Indians to escape. This was done, and closing toward a center, the two savages were found in a "buffalo wallow," a depression in the ground made by the buffaloes which formed a very good rifle pit. After being addressed in their own language, they refused to surrender and were shot. General Sully afterward had their heads cut off; and when the command left camp next morning, they graced two pointed stakes on the bank of the river, placed there as a warning to all straggling Indians bent on murder or mayhem.

The feeling manifested by General Sully on the occasion of Captain Fielner's death was intense. A brave officer, a scientific scholar, and a gentleman of rare social qualities he had won the kindlier feelings of his associates in rank, and was respected by all. His untimely death was sincerely mourned by the whole command.

Death by the hand of the enemy had seldom touched that little army—so seldom, that when a companion failed to answer at roll call, his absence was felt. The only other officer killed during the three years of General Sully's operations against the Indians was Lieutenant Thomas K. Leavitt, Company B, Sixth Iowa Cavalry. At the battle of Whitestone Hill in September, 1863, after the Indians had been completely routed, Lieutenant Leavitt went through their deserted camp on foot, his horse having been shot from under him; and finding a buffalo robe, raised it with the point of his saber, revealing an Indian and squaw, who sprang upon him so suddenly that he had no opportunity to defend himself, and with their knives, stabbed him in several places. Darkness came on, and separated from his companions, stripped of his clothing, and wounded mortally he was all night exposed to bitter cold. Despite his wounds, he crawled over the ground fully a half mile. He was discovered next morning and conveyed to camp, where he died soon after. A fine, young man of superior education and from a wealthy family, he relinquished a lucrative position in a bank and enlisted as a private, but was soon promoted to a lieutenancy. When he died, he was acting Adjutant General on General Sully's staff.

The emigrant train to be escorted by General Sully's command came across from Minnesota and was joined at a point on the Missouri River about four hundred miles above Sioux City. Here the whole party crossed to the west bank of the Missouri, where they went into camp and remained long enough to recruit their jaded animals preparatory to a long and fatiguing march into an almost unknown wilderness jealously guarded by a savage foe.

During this halt, Fort Rice, now one of the most important fortifications on the Missouri River, was built, and when the march was resumed, a considerable portion of the command was left to garrison it.

At this time, General Sully learned that all the tribes of the Sioux nation had congregated in the vicinity of Knife River, determined to resist his passage through their country. They felt confident that their superior numbers would enable them to annihilate the whole expedition and gain a rich booty in horses and goods, to say nothing of the hundreds of scalp locks they hoped to win as trophies of their prowess.

About the middle of July, the expedition took up its march westward, and after several days reached Heart River. Meantime, information had been received from Indians employed as scouts that the enemy had gathered in strong force at a place called Ta-ka-a-ku-ta, or Deer Woods, about eighty miles to the northwest, and a distance from the proposed route of the expedition. Accordingly, General Sully ordered the emigrant train and heavy army wagons corralled, rifle pits were dug, and as the emigrants were generally well-armed, it was deemed necessary to leave only a small number of cavalry to protect them in case of attack.

Putting the balance of the command into light marching order, leaving behind tents and all other articles not absolutely necessary, the little band of determined men started for the enemy's camp.

Although the Indians were aware of the contemplated attack, the celerity of General Sully's movements were such that troops arrived within sight of their camp at least twenty-four hours sooner than they thought possible the march could be accomplished. By so doing he took the Indians by surprise; they not having time, as is their custom, to remove their property and women and children beyond the reach of danger.

I was present with this body of Indians when the white soldiers—my countrymen—came in sight. Alternating between hope and fear, my feelings can be better imagined than described. I hoped for rescue, yet feared disaster and death.

At one o'clock in the afternoon, the fight commenced, and raged with increasing fury until night closed on the scene of conflict, leaving the troops masters of the field and in possession of the Indian camp.

Early in the day, I, with the women and children and old men, and such property as could be gathered in our hasty flight, was sent off so as to be out of the way and not impede the flight of the Indians in case of defeat.

This was a terrible blow to the Indians. Nearly eight thousand of them were gathered there, and their village with all their property (except their horses and dogs) including all the stores of provisions they had gathered for the winter were lost. Now with neither food nor shelter and driven into a barren, desolate region devoid of game, death from starvation seemed inevitable.

Early next morning pursuit was commenced, but after a march of about five miles was abandoned, as the country beyond was impassable for cavalry. Returning to the scene of the previous day's battle, General Sully spent several hours in destroying the property abandoned by the Indians in their flight. Lodge poles were piled together and fired, and into the flames was cast furs, robes, tents, provisions, and everything that fell into the soldiers' hands.

That night the command camped about six miles from, but within sight of, the battleground, going into camp early in the afternoon. Picket guards were stationed on the hills, three at a post, and soon after the camp was thrown into commotion by the appearance of one of the guards dashing toward camp at the full speed of his horse with Indians in pursuit. His companions, worn out with the arduous service of the preceding three days, had laid down to sleep, and before the one remaining on guard could give the alarm, a body of Indians was close upon them. Discharging his rifle to arouse his companions, he had barely time to reach his horse and escape. The bodies of the other two were found next day horribly mutilated; and that night, being within sight of the battleground, the firelight revealed the forms of a large body of savages dancing around the burning ruins of their own homes.

Returning to Heart River, General Sully took the emigrants again in charge and resumed the march toward Idaho.

Traversing a country diversified and beautiful as the sun ever shone upon, presenting at every turn pictures of natural beauty such as no artist ever represented on canvas, the expedition at last struck the "Mauvais Terra" or Bad Lands, a region of the most wildly desolate terrain conceivable. No description by writer nor brush of painter can give the faintest idea of its awful desolation.

As the command halted upon the confines of this desert, the mind reverted to political descriptions of the infernal regions reached in other days.

The Bad Lands of Dakota extend from the confluence of the Yellowstone and Missouri Rivers toward the southwest, a distance of about one hundred miles, and are from twenty-five to forty miles in width. The foot of white man had never trod these wilds before.

The first day's march into this desert carried the expedition only ten miles, consuming ten hours of time and leaving the forces four miles from, and within sight of, the camp they left in the morning. On the seventh of August the advance guard was attacked in the afternoon by a large party of Indians. After a toilsome march of many days, a valley in the wilderness was reached, which offered an opportunity for rest. And here the first vegetation was found for the famished horses. In this valley the troops set up camp; the advance guard was brought back, having suffered some from the attack of the ambushed savages.

Next day commenced one of the most memorable battles ever fought with Indians in the whole experience of the Government. The whole Dakota nation, including the supposed friendly tribes, was concentrated there and numbered fully eight thousand warriors. Opposed to them was a mere handful, comparatively, of white men. But they were led by one skilled in war and who knew the foe he had to contend against.

For three days the fight raged, and, finally, on the night of the third day, and after a toilsome march of eleven days through the Bad Lands, the command reached a broad, open country where the savages made a final, desperate stand to drive the invaders back. They were the wild Dakotans, who had seen but little of the white settlements and had a contemptuous opinion. But a new lesson was now to be learned, and it cost them dearly. They had seen guns large and small, but the little mountain howitzers, from which shells were sent among them, they could not comprehend. The Indian scouts accompanying the expedition were asked if all the wagons "shot twice." Terrible punishment was inflicted upon the Indians in that three days' fight.

At the close of the second day, the brigade wagon master reported that he had discovered the tracks of a white woman, and believed the Indians held one captive. This was the first intimation General Sully received of my captivity, and, not having received from the western posts any report of captures by Indians, thought it must be some half-breed woman who wore the footgear of civilization.

But the sympathetic nature of that brave, noble General was stirred to its depths when his Indian scouts reported that they had talked with the hostile foe, and they had tauntingly said, "we have a white woman captive."

The Indians were badly whipped, and having accomplished that portion of his mission, General Sully went forward with his emigrant train to the Yellowstone River and beyond.

Early in October the command arrived opposite Fort Rice and went into camp. The tents of the little band of white warriors were hardly pitched before word came that Captain Fisk, with a large party of emigrants and a small escort of soldiers, had been attacked by a large party of Indians, who had corralled the train so it could not move. They were on the defensive and confident of holding out until relief arrived. They were about one hundred and eighty miles distant, and the sympathetic nature of the veteran, while it condemned the action of his junior officer, thrilled with an earnest desire to save the women and children of that apparently doomed train.

A detail of men from each company of the command was made, and Captain Fisk and his train of emigrants were rescued from their perilous situation. Here was proof positive of the fact that a white woman was held captive by the Indians; and while every man would have been willing to risk his life for her rescue, and many applications were made to the General for permission to go out on expeditions for that purpose, he had already adopted such measures to secure her release.

Friendly Indians who had accompanied the expedition were sent out to visit the various tribes and to assure them of an earnest desire on the part of the whites for peace. All were invited to meet at Fort Sully to make a treaty. The result was that about the latter part of October the vicinity of the fort presented an unusual appearance of animation. Several groups had arrived in anticipation of the big feast that had hitherto preceded all talks. Their disappointment may be imagined when they were told that no talk would be had, nor any feast given, until they brought in the white woman. Their protestations that she was not their captive and that they could not get her from the band who held her were of no avail, and, at length, Tall Soldier, who was thought to be friendly, called for volunteers to go with him for the white woman. About one hundred Indians agreed, and assurance was given that they would get the captive, even at the expense of a fight.

Weeks of painful suspense passed; then an Indian brought a letter from the captive woman in which warning was given of an intent to capture the fort and murder the garrison. The warning was acted upon; and when, on the twelfth day of December,[1] a large body of Indians appeared on the bluffs overlooking the fort, that little band of not more than

[1] The correct date was December 9.

two hundred men was prepared to give them a warm reception should they come with hostile intent. Not only were guns in prime condition but every heart beat with high resolve.

When the cavalcade drew up in front of the fort and the captive woman with about twelve of her immediate savage attendants had passed through the gates, they were ordered closed, shutting out the main body and leaving them exposed to a raking fire from the guns in the bastions.

But no attack was made. The Indians seemed to know that the little band of soldiers was prepared, and went quietly into camp on an island opposite the fort. Next day a council was held and the terms of the captive's surrender agreed upon. Three unserviceable horses, to replace ponies left with the Oglalas by the Blackfeet, as a pledge for the captive's return; also fifty dollars worth of presents, some provisions, and a promise of a treaty when General Sully should return. The Indians remained about the fort nearly two weeks, and during that time they made efforts to induce the captive woman to leave the fort and visit them at their lodges, doubtless with the design of recapturing her. After giving the captive some presents, they then bade adieu. Two months later they returned, apparently very much disappointed when they found the captive had left for her home.

They were soon again upon the warpath.

DEDICATED TO MRS. FANNY KELLY

By a Soldier

In early youth, far in the distant west,
With gentle steps the fragrant fields you pressed;
Then joy rebounded in thy youthful heart,
Nor thought of care, or trouble, bore no part.
The morn of life, whose sky seems ever bright,
And distant hills are tinged with crimson light,
When hope, bright hope, by glowing fancies driven,
Fill'd thy young heart with raptured thoughts of heaven.
'Twas there, 'neath yonder glorious western sky,
Where noble forests wave their heads on high,
And gentle zephyrs, filled with rich perfume,
Swept o'er vast prairies in undying bloom;
And there where silvery lakes and rippling streams,
Go murmuring through the hills and valleys green,
And birds sing gayly, as they soar along,
In gentle notes, their ever-welcome song.
'Twas there was passed thy youthful life away,
And all became a dread reality;
Then woo'd and wedded to the one you loved,
As partner of thy life all else above;
To share thy brightest hopes, or gloomy fears,
Or mingle in thy smiles, or gushing tears;
To be to thee a constant bosom friend,
Faithful and true till life's last hours should end.
Those days and years so pleasantly passed by,
No tears of grief—thy bosom knew no sigh;
But, ah! those days, those halcyon days, are past,
Those sunny hours, they were too sweet to last!
For far out o'er the broadest prairie plain,
Onward you pressed a distant home to gain.

Days, even weeks, so pleasantly passed o'er,
That mem'ry brought back those sweet days of yore;
Those days of thy youth for which you did sigh,
But ne'er did ye think that some soon should die.
For days of sadness, those days that come to all,
From the humblest cot to the palace hall,
When gathering darkness cloud the clear, blue sky,
Our brightest prospects all in ruin lie.
While gathering round the camp at close of day,
As the sun shed forth her last but lingering ray,
The war whoop of the Sioux Indian band
Was heard; "They come," and all surrounded stand.
A moment more, and then around thee lay,
As the dark smoke had cleared itself away,
The lifeless forms of those in horror slain,
And thou, alas! the only one remain.
No bosom friend, no counselor is near,
To sooth thy troubled breast, or quell thy fear.
Those dearest by all earthly ties are fled,
And you, a captive, stand among the dead;
For months in bondage to this savage band,
With none to rescue from his cruel hand,
To rove with them o'er prairies far and wild,
Far from thy husband and thy murdered child.
No star of hope, nor sun's resplendent light,
Sends down one gleam upon this fearful night;
No power to pierce the dark and hidden gloom,
That veils the heart while in this earthly tomb.
But, lo! a change, a wondrous change, to thee!
Once held a captive, but now from bondage free.
To great Jehovah reigns; His arm is strong,
He sets the captive free, though waiteth long,
And turns the darkest hours of midnight gloom,
Into the effulgent brightness of noon.

W.S.V.H.

EPILOGUE

For FANNY KELLY, the ordeal of her captivity was, without doubt, the most traumatic experience of her life. Yet, sad to say, after her return to freedom there was still more tragedy and personal problems to overcome.

As Fanny notes near the end of her narrative, her husband, Josiah, died of cholera on July 28, 1867, and just a few days later Fanny faced alone the birth and rearing of a son, whom she named after his father. Then, as she was casting about for ways to make a living while at the same time preparing a manuscript of her terror and privation, she was contacted by the Larimers who invited her and the baby to join them at Sherman Station, Wyoming Territory. It would turn out to be a disastrous move for all concerned.

After Sarah and William Larimer were reunited at Deer Creek Station less than a week after the attack, Sarah nursed her wounded husband back to health. Then the little family moved to Fort Laramie where they decided to engage in the photographic business. With borrowed money, William Larimer ordered from Leavenworth the replacement supplies for those lost in the wagon train attack. However, because of the constant threat of Indian hostilities, it took almost two months for the order to arrive. Then, in April 1865, the Larimers left Fort

Laramie for Denver where they established another photography studio. Apparently, they were not happy there and soon transferred their business back to Wyoming Territory, locating in the little railroad town of Sherman Station between Cheyenne and Laramie. There, in addition to their studio, they also ran a general store, with a wide range of merchandise including alcohol by the bottle or barrel. Furthermore, they bought and sold railroad ties and cordwood, and for a time William Larimer appeared to have had an interest in a Cheyenne saloon, as well as a star-route mail contract and a stage line that ran daily coaches between Point of Rocks (near present Rock Springs) and South Pass City, an aspiring mining camp near the Continental Divide and the Overland Trail.

We do know that after arriving in Sherman Station, Fanny worked briefly as a washerwoman, an occupation that was not uncommon for women in the nineteenth century. Then the record skips to October 1870 when Fanny filed a lawsuit against both Larimers, her "false friends," in the District Court of Allen County, Kansas, after she had been to Washington to present her claims against the Government and the Indians.

In her suit, Fanny alleged that in December 1865, she and Sarah Larimer agreed to prepare a joint memoir of their experiences in captivity, to be published under both names. Furthermore, she stated that in May 1869, when the narrative was nearly completed, Sarah Larimer secretly took the manuscript to Philadelphia and had it published in her own name, as her own work, thus depriving Fanny, the true author, of credit, reputation, and profit; and that William Larimer had conspired with his wife in this fraud.

The book in question seems to be Sarah L. Larimer's *The Capture and Escape; Or, Life among the Sioux*, which Claxton, Remsen and Haffelfinger of Philadelphia published in 1870, and in which Larimer had included, "For want of room in this volume, which has already exceeded the limits originally contemplated, I am compelled to omit the highly interesting experience of Mrs. Kelly, but issue it in a book entitled, 'Mrs. Kelly's Experience Among the Indians.'" Apparently, Claxton had actually printed the second book, but had not bound it, and Kelly was able to insist ultimately on the destruction of all copies.

When the case came to trial, the Larimers argued as one of their defenses, that Sarah as a *feme covert*, (a married woman without a trade or business at the time of the agreement), could not legally enter into a valid contract. The verdict favored Fanny who won a judgment for $5,000. The Larimers appealed; the court's decision was reversed, and the case remanded for further proceedings, largely on the grounds that Kelly had not proven the value of the manuscript. After considerable legal maneuvering and a change of venue to the Woodson District

Court, Fanny won again, although the judgment was for but $285.50. Once more the Larimers attacked the decision—this time on the grounds that one of the jurors had been drinking hard liquor on the morning of the verdict. But the Kansas Supreme Court failed to sustain the contention, and the legal battle continued on until the late summer of 1876 when the parties reached a private settlement and the case was dismissed at Kelly's costs, which one writer estimates to have been $2,000, an enormous sum for that day, and which seems not to have been paid, or at least not fully paid to the court.[1]

Fanny Kelly's own narrative of her captivity was printed early in 1871 by Witstach, Baldwin & Company of Cincinnati and quickly republished in that same year by the Mutual Publishing Company of Hartford, Connecticut. There is such a similarity between many sentences and even paragraphs

[1] Part of the court record, including many depositions, is contained on microfilm of Fanny Kelly *vs.* Sarah Larimer, *et al.*, 1869–77, Franklin County Court Case File No. 1780, Kansas Historical Society, Topeka. See also Sarah L. Larimer, *et al.*, *vs.* Fanny Kelly, 10 *Kansas Reports*, pp. 298–313; William J. Larimer *vs.* Fanny Kelly, 13 *Kansas Reports*, pp. 64–65; Alan W. Farley, "An Indian Captivity and Its Legal Aftermath," *Kansas Historical Quarterly*, XXI (Winter, 1954), pp. 247–56. Allusions to the economic interests of the Larimers may be found in Larimer, *Capture and Escape*, pp. 249–52; also in Jonathan Luse's testimony (Case File No. 1780) as well as in John Bratt, *Trails of Yesterday* (Lincoln, Nebr., reprint, 1980), p. 156. The latter is not always accurate in detail, but includes an example of Sarah Larimer's photographic work.

appearing in Fanny's work and Larimer's *Capture and Escape* that it seems safe to conclude that the two books must have been the product of one author or of an early joint authorship.

If the depositions of witnesses for the defendants are to be believed, Kelly's book was virtually identical with the suppressed book allegedly authored by Sarah Larimer, a copy of which was bound and exhibited at the trial. Fanny charged that Sarah had "surreptitiously taken" the manuscript of her narrative while they were living together in Sherman Station. Sarah, in turn, alleged that Fanny's draft had perished when her Ellsworth, Kansas, home burned and that Fanny subsequently had "feloniously abstracted and purloined" the printed proof sheets of Sarah's book from Sarah's room. The complete testimony of witnesses on behalf of Kelly has not survived, but the verdict of the jurors indicate their belief that Kelly had been wronged and that both the published and suppressed Larimer books were either the products of joint authorship, or in the case of the one withdrawn from publication, perhaps Fanny's own work with some rewriting and refinements added by an assistant.

With this present edition, Fanny's book has gone through eleven editions or printings, two of which were in Canada. It is worth mentioning that the 1880 printing was done by Donnelley, Gassette & Loyd (a predecessor company), and the 1891 printing by R. R. Donnelley & Sons Company.

Fanny's story made for popular reading. It was clear-cut drama, with a blend of tragedy, pathos, savage cruelty, but withal a seemingly happy ending for the gritty, young heroine. It carried with it the magic of the Old West during a time when an increasingly impersonal industrial, urban society seemed to be submerging the individual.

Interestingly, the record shows that on September 27, 1871, Fanny Kelly registered in the Library of Congress Copyright Office the following book title: *Afterwards: or Life and Trials Subsequent to My Captivity Among the Sioux, with an Account of the Litigation Concerning My History, in which Truth is Stranger than Fiction.* It was never published, but the title alone may well have indicated the state of her mind at the time.

By comparison, Larimer's book has been reprinted only once, and this time without the promise to bring out a book on Mrs. Kelly's experience among the Indians. Both Fanny's and Sarah's accounts are included in the 1976 Garland series of Indian captivity stories.

Although in some ways the Larimer book might be considered more descriptive than Kelly's, Sarah's narrative proved far less popular, probably because her two days in captivity were not long enough on which to build a sustained personal account.

William J. Larimer was moved by his long association with litigation to study law and the 1880 Dakota Territorial Census listed him as living alone as an "attorney-at-law" in the Black Hills settlement of Lead City. In 1888 some members of Congress became aware that the Larimers had separated. At the time, they were negotiating a bill to compensate Sarah for the "valuable services" she rendered by giving important information to the army in 1864 on the "evil designs of hostile Indians." The bill ultimately was passed and the Treasury directed a $5,000 check to Tacoma, Washington Territory, where she was then living.[2]

Fanny Kelly educated her little son in private schools and he ultimately grew up to become a banker in Jefferson, Oklahoma. Fanny settled in Washington, D.C., and on May 6, 1880, she married William F. Gordon, a Kansas journalist, who specialized in ghostwriting for prominent Americans. Reputedly, she found employment with the Federal Government in the nation's capital, but the editors have been unable to determine with what agency or office. She did accumulate money, invested extensively in real estate, including the Calvert Mansion in Riversdale, Maryland, which had belonged to the son of the sixth Lord Baltimore, and inherited the old Wiggins homestead back in Geneva.

[2]A proposal to compensate Sarah had been introduced as early as 1885, but not until October, 1888, did a private bill pass on her behalf. See Senate *Report* 1591, 50th Cong., 1st Sess. [Serial 2524]; 25 *U.S. Statutes at Large*, Private Acts, pp. 37–38. The Records of the Bureau of Accounts (Record Group 39), National Archives, show that Sarah Larimer was paid $5,000 by Indian Warrant No. 377.

Fanny held membership in the women's branch of the Grand Army of the Republic as well as the Nurses' Union, and she established a fine reputation for her private charities and work among women. In spite of the trials of her captivity, she seemed to have acquired an affection for Indians, and entertained some of their dignitaries when they visited Washington.

Her little granddaughter, Fanny, had not yet been born when she died on November 15, 1904, of a cerebral hemorrhage, presumably at her home at 914 Eighth Street Northwest, and was buried in the Glenwood Cemetery in the heart of the District of Columbia.[3]

CLARK C. SPENCE
MARY LEE SPENCE

---

[3]Obituary notices appeared in the Washington *Post*, November 18, 1904, and the *Iola Register* (Kansas), December 19, 1904. The former is brief; the latter is inaccurate. The adopted daughter of Josiah Kelly, Jr., Mrs. Jane Foley of Pond Creek, Oklahoma, has given a few details of the Kelly family in letters to Randy Brown of Douglas, Wyoming, but notes that the family lost a number of interesting documents when a flash flood inundated their basement. William F. Gordon may have been the former editor of the *North Kansas*, a newspaper published in Hiawatha, Kansas, from 1872 to 1878.

Appendix

TO THE SENATORS AND MEMBERS
OF THE HOUSE OF
REPRESENTATIVES OF CONGRESS

Your memorialist, Mrs. Fanny Kelly, a citizen of the United States, and residing in the State of Kansas, respectfully petitioning your Honorable bodies, represents:

That during the summer months of the year 1864, your memorialist, in company with her husband, Josiah Kelly, (now deceased), and a party consisting of Wm. J. Larimer, wife and child, Mr. Sharp, Mr. Taylor, Mr. Wakefield, and the adopted daughter of your memorialist, Mary J. Hurley, left different portions of the State of Kansas to go to Montana Territory. The party united at a point west of the northwestern border of Kansas, and journeyed together. Your memorialist and her husband had in their possession, and owned at the time, certain valuable goods and chattels (a full exhibit of which, with the market value thereof, is hereto attached and made part hereof, marked exhibit "A"). Your memorialist's husband was removing to Bannock City, Montana, with these goods, with a view to enter into trade.

On the 12th day of July, 1864, our party had reached a point some 80 miles west of Fort Laramie. While encamped a mixed party of Indians came into our camp, and deporting themselves in a friendly manner (by shaking hands and other demonstrations of friendship) asked us for supper. During its preparation, the number of Indians increased to nearly one hundred. They were composed of O-gal-lal-lah, and Yank-ton Sioux, Black-feet, and Rees and Gro-rout Indians (the latter called "Farmer Indians"), also some Hunc-pa-pas.

It had been represented to our party by the Military Commanders along the route of travel, that there was no danger to be apprehended from Indians; that we were

272

entirely secure from attack, and we continued our journey without any fear.

While these preparations for supper were being made, the Indians, who had asked our hospitality, fired upon the men of our party. Mr. Sharp, Mr. Taylor and the Negro boy fell dead at the first fire. Mr. Wakefield and Mr. Larimer were dangerously wounded, and hobbled off to the bushes. Your memorialist's husband was gathering wood at the time, and succeeded in escaping without injury. The Indians then surrounded the wagons for the purpose of plunder. They sacked the wagons, burned and destroyed what they could not carry away, and took the survivors of the party prisoners. Your memorialist was dragged rudely from one of the wagons and severely injured, from which she suffered for many months. Your memorialist was then taken into captivity, and was forced to become the squaw of one of the O-gal-lal-lah Chiefs, who treated her in a manner too horrible to mention, and during her captivity was passed from Chief to Chief, and treated in a similar manner. Your memorialist kept as full a memoranda of her captivity, and the incidents thereof, as was possible, and has, since her return to her home, reduced the same to a narrative form, embracing the entire period from date of capture to date of release. Your memorialist begs to refer your Honorable bodies to this narrative, as showing in detail something of her sufferings, privations and perils, and especially as presenting the evidence of her valuable services to the United States troops, which after her capture, entered the warpath against the Indians.

During her captivity, which lasted from July 12, 1864, until December 9, 1864, your memorialist acquired somewhat of the language of the Indians, which numbered two or three thousand, banded for plunder and murder, and was enabled to understand their plans and designs. These your memorialist contrived to communicate, from time to time, to emigrant and freight trains, and to troops. And your memorialist would especially call attention to her valuable service rendered the garrison at Fort Sully, which, it will be seen, contributed largely to saving that garrison from total massacre. Your memorialist refers to her narrative as exhibit "B," and to letters and other evidences herewith submitted to show your Honorable bodies the truth of her statement.

Your memorialist says that some of her captors claimed to be *annuity* Indians, and boasted that they were drawing money and clothing from the white man, while at the same time they had certain of the whites prisoners. The circumstances showing that some of my captors were *annuity* Indians, appear in my narrative.

Your memorialist respectfully urges upon your Honorable bodies, that she is now in destitute circumstances; that all her earthly effects were taken and destroyed by the Indians; that her husband has since died, leaving her helpless and poor; that her adopted daughter was cruelly murdered by her captors, and your memorialist is now alone in the world. She urges that her services to emigrants, traders and United States troops, while she was a captive, often sacrificing her own comfort, and endangering her life, and certainly prolonging her captivity, to render these services, will surely commend her cause to your Honorable bodies. Your memorialist asks some compensation in such sum as may seem mete, and she will, as in duty bound, ever pray.

FANNY KELLY